C000259747

# British Cars of the Late Thirties 1935-1939

edited by Bart H. Vanderveen

**ISBN 0 85429 561 5**

A **FOULIS** Motoring Book

First published, in the Auto Library Series, by Frederick Warne, 1973
Reprinted 1979, 1986



*Published by:*
**Haynes Publishing Group**
Sparkford, Nr. Yeovil,
Somerset BA22 7JJ

**Haynes Publications Inc,**
861 Lawrence Drive, Newbury Park,
California 91320 USA.

**Other titles in this series**

Cross-Country Cars from 1945
Half-Tracks
Fire and Crash Vehicles from 1950
Fire-Fighting Vehicles 1840-1950
Trucks of the Sixties and Seventies
Wreckers and Recovery Vehicles
Passenger Vehicles 1893-1940
Buses and Coaches from 1940

American Cars of the 1930s
American Cars of the 1940s
American Cars of the 1950s
American Cars of the 1960s
American Cars of the 1970s

American Trucks of the Late Thirties

British Cars of the Early Thirties
British Cars of the Early Forties
British Cars of the Late Forties
British Cars of the Early Fifties
British Cars of the Late Fifties
British Cars of the Early Sixties
British Cars of the Late Sixties

Motorcycles from 1945

# INTRODUCTION

Following its companion volume *British Cars of the Early Thirties—1930–34*, this book covers a large number of cars produced in the United Kingdom from 1935 until 1939, when the second World War started. During this period the British Motor Industry produced a great variety of great cars, ranging from small but well-developed economy models to what were justly claimed to be the world's best. Included were popular family saloons, sports cars of many sizes, super-luxury limousines, as well as tough medium-sized cars aimed at the world's export markets.

Most of them were typically British, with their pros and cons. Whilst exceptionally well finished and equipped, and ideal for operation 'at home' where roads were smooth but winding and steep gradients abundant, they were often eschewed by foreign car buyers, even within the Empire, who for the same money could buy more powerful and sturdier cars, especially of American origin. Well-known historian Michael Sedgwick, giving his views about this state of things in his informative book *Cars of the 1930s*, aptly put it like this "... serious attempts were made to woo the colonials away from their Chevrolets and Buicks in the 1930s, but Hillman's 'Wizard' and 'Hawk' were more expensive to make, and offered nothing a Chevrolet did not have except leather upholstery (an unnecessary frill in the Outback) and sliding roofs, which let in dust. If the later six-cylinder Vauxhalls did rather better, it was because of their American-based specifications, which rendered patriotism painless. In other White areas of the Empire, the demand was even less. Canada had her own industry, turning out American cars in vast numbers at almost American prices, while South Africa had no sentimental ties with Britain which would prompt an Afrikaner to choose a Humber 'Snipe' in preference to a Buick.

"In 'black' Africa the proconsuls might have graduated from Crossleys to Humber 'Pullmans' and the larger Armstrong Siddeleys, but a district commissioner in Kenya or Uganda, confronted with dust clouds, monsoons, and dirt roads, wanted no part of wood-framed bodies, opening screens and indifferent service. There was no meal for termites in a 'turret-top' Chevrolet, and the Ford's transverse suspension was at its best in the rough. The equivalent of £500 would buy a Chrysler or Buick. What Britain sold abroad was what she could make best—small sports cars and luxury carriages".

For all that, British family cars of the thirties had a certain uniqueness, partly brought about by the peculiar horsepower taxation system, based on an absurd and hypothetical RAC-designed formula which had little if anything to do with actual power output. It could also be argued that during this decade the United Kingdom was more isolated from the rest of the world than at any other time in automotive history, which inevitably had its effects on designs and developments.

**Piet Olyslager MSIA MSAE KIVI**

**1935** Motor vehicle production in the United Kingdom during the 1935 calendar year broke all previous records, with a total of well over 400,000, namely 325,192 private cars, 91,707 trucks and buses and some 9,100 tractors. About a quarter of a million people were now employed in the motor manufacturing and repair industries. Export figures for 1935 showed a healthy increase with 54,520 cars finding their way overseas, valued at £6,368,875. Commonwealth countries were the principal export markets but in a relatively small, although quite near, country like the Netherlands most British cars were available. A total of 13,563 cars and car chassis was imported, valued at over £2.1 million. Motor vehicles in use in the United Kingdom in September, 1935, numbered 2,034,589, about three quarters of these being private cars. During the calendar year ending December 1935, there were 413,765 new vehicle registrations; of these 281,388 were private cars and just under seven thousand hackneys.

4A AC 16/66

4A: **AC** (Acedes) offered 16/56 and 16/66 models. An early Sports Four-seater of the latter range is shown. It had a 1990-cc (65 × 100 mm) three-carburettor 66-bhp OHC engine, rated at 15·7 HP. Wheelbase was 9 ft 7 in, tyre size 5·00-19. In the 1935 Monte Carlo Rally three ACs entered and all finished, including Miss M. Allen, the first British woman competitor in the rally, who drove an AC from Umea, Sweden.
4B: **Alvis** Firebird range comprised four-seater Sports, Saloon (shown) and Drophead Coupé models. The 9 ft 10½ in wheelbase chassis was also available for special coachwork, at £410. The engine was an 1842-cc (73 × 110 mm) OHV Four, rated at 13·22 HP, actual output being 61 bhp at 4300 rpm. Six-cylinder models were the Silver Eagle Sixteen, Crested Eagle and Speed Twenty, priced at up to £850.

4B Alvis Firebird

5A: **Armstrong Siddeley** offered Twelve-Six (shown), Fifteen, Twenty, Long Twenty and Siddeley Special models. Later in the year a new model, the Seventeen, was introduced. The 1935 Fifteen had permanently-fitted hydraulic jacks. All had six-cylinder engines and self-changing gearboxes. The 4·96-litre Special models featured twin SU carburettors.

Thousands of enthusiastic owners have proved the quality and long life of the Armstrong Siddeley Twelve-Six. Equipped with first class coachwork, roomy accommodation and an engine of Aircraft quality, all combine to make this the best money-value obtainable in a light car with large car comfort.

ARMSTRONG SIDDELEY MOTORS LIMITED, COVENTRY
LONDON: 10 OLD BOND STREET, W.1 MANCHESTER: 35 KING STREET WEST

Official tests and ordinary running experience confirm— It pays to buy a British car.

5A Armstrong Siddeley Twelve-Six

5B Austin Seven

5B: **Austin** Seven Two-seater in service dress. This was basically the 1934/35 civilian model, with only minor modifications. Nearly 900 of this version were delivered to the British Army. It superseded the earlier type which had military pattern bodywork and was popularly known as 'the pram'.

5C: **Austin** Seven Ruby De Luxe Saloon was one of a wide range of models in this popular economy range. Like the other Austin ranges the bodywork had been entirely restyled for the 1935 model year (commencing July 1934). It was generally more rounded, with slightly sloping radiator grille and shell painted to match the coachwork, longer bonnet with ventilator doors matching the scuttle ventilator, radiator filler under the bonnet, strengthened and lowered frame and other improvements. The Ruby had a 747·5-cc (56×76 mm) 12-bhp side-valve four-cylinder rubber-mounted engine, rated at 7·8 HP, with four-speed synchromesh gearbox. Wheelbase was 6 ft 9 in, tyre size 4·00-17. It cost £120; the basic version, without sliding roof, was available at £112.

5D: **Austin** Seven Two-Seater for 1935 selling season was initially a continuation of the earlier square style, designated Opal. The Opal and the four-seater Open Road Tourer, in fact, retained the 1933/34 high frame until well into the 1935 model year. The Two-seater shown is of the later type, registered towards the end of 1935. The Nippy and Speedy Sports Two-seaters were also continued with the earlier body styling.

5C Austin Seven

5D Austin Seven

## 1935

6A Austin Ten-Four

6B Austin Sixteen-Six

6C Austin Eighteen-Six

6D Avon Standard 10 HP

---

6A: **Austin** Ten-Four Lichfield Saloon looked much like the Seven Ruby but had four doors and was larger with one foot more wheelbase and overall length. It had an 1125-cc (63·5 × 89 mm) 20-bhp L-head Four engine, rated at 9·9 HP. Body style variants included the Colwyn Cabriolet, Clifton Two-seater and Ripley Sports.

6B: **Austin** Sixteen-Six could be ordered with Hayes self-selector automatic gearbox at extra cost. Picture shows a car thus equipped being presented to the Austin Motor Co in 1961 by Mr R. J. Wyatt, Secretary of the Vintage Austin Register.

6C: **Austin** Eighteen-Six looked similar to the Sixteen-Six, the reason being that the Sixteen could be supplied with either 2249-cc or 2510-cc engine. Both had 111-mm stroke but bore was 65·5 mm and 69·5 mm respectively, giving a treasury rating of 15·9 and 17·9 HP. Wheelbase was 10 ft or 9 ft 4 in, depending on body style. Shown is a York Limousine with 17·9 HP ('Eighteen') engine and long wheelbase.

6D: **Avon Standard** 10 HP Coupé was built by the New Avon Body Company Ltd of Warwick, based on a 7 ft 10 in wheelbase Standard. Inside the body there was room for driver, passenger and two small children and there was a dicky seat which would accommodate two medium size passengers if necessary. Engine was the Standard 1343-cc (63·5 × 106 mm) 32-bhp side-valve Four. Optional at a small extra cost was the Standard 12 HP 1608-cc (69·5 × 106 mm) engine with twin RAG carburettors and a higher gear ratio.

7A: **Avon Standard** 16 HP Open Two-Four-Seater Sports was based on the 9 ft 2 in wheelbase Standard Sixteen chassis with 2143-cc (65·5 × 106 mm) 48-bhp six-cylinder side-valve engine. Optional extras included a 20 HP engine (Standard Twenty, 2664-cc, 60-bhp), ACE wheel discs, spare wheel cover, etc. Like the 10-12 HP models it had a DWS permanent four-wheel jacking system as standard equipment. Also available in the 16 HP range were a Close-Coupled Coupé and a pillarless Saloon called the Waymaker 1.

7B: **Bentley** produced one standard chassis, the 3½-Litre with 10 ft 6 in wheelbase. It cost £1100 and was used by various specialist coach builders. The company itself offered three types of complete cars, viz. an Open Tourer at £1380, a Four-door Saloon at £1460 and a Drophead Coupé at £1485. The engine was a 3669-cc (82·5 × 114 mm) OHV six-cylinder, rated at 25·3 HP. Actual bhp output was not disclosed. This Saloon has a body by Park Ward.

7A Avon Standard 16 HP

7B Bentley 3½-Litre

7C British Salmson 12/55

7C: **British Salmson** 12/55 (shown) and 12/65 models were offered by the British Salmson Aero Engines Ltd. Both models had a 1470-cc (69 × 98 mm) twin-OHC four-cylinder engine, rated at 11·9 HP. The power output of the 12/55 was 55 bhp at 4500 rpm, that of the 12/65 was 65 at 5500. All had servo-assisted brakes and four-wheel jacking system as standard equipment.

8A-B: **Brough** Superior was Hudson-engined high-performance car designed by George Brough. Mr Brough, of Nottingham, was well-known as the designer of the famous Brough motorcycle and as holder of many awards for motoring events. The Brough Car was originally intended to be for his own use ('for my own smoking' as he put it) but in 1935 quantity production commenced, albeit on a very small scale. The eight-cylinder side-valve engine had a capacity of 4168 cc (76×114 mm) and an output of 125 bhp at 4000 rpm. The Dual Purpose car had bodywork by Atcherly of Birmingham and sold at £695.
8C: **BSA** offered 10 HP and Light Six models, all with the Daimler Fluid Flywheel four-speed transmission. The two types differed mainly in engine specification. The 10 HP had an 1185-cc (63×95 mm) side-valve Four, developing 28 bhp. The Light Six engine was an OHV 1378-cc (57×90 mm) unit with a power output of 34 bhp. By October, 1935, a Ten Saloon De Luxe with 1330-cc (63·5×105 mm) was also available.
8D: **Campbell/Rolls-Royce** Bluebird World Land Speed Record car. In the guise shown here it was powered by a $36\frac{1}{2}$-litre 12-cylinder Rolls-Royce aero-engine, developing about 2500 bhp. The car, with which Sir Malcolm Campbell eventually broke through the 300 mph barrier in 1935, weighed close to five tons and had dual rear tyres to combat wheelspin. Much of the design work had been done by Reid Railton. Visible in the background in this Reigate, Surrey, showroom are a Triumph Gloria Southern Cross Two-seater and a Rover Sports Saloon.

8A Brough Superior

8B Brough Superior

8C BSA 10 HP

8D Campbell/Rolls-Royce Bluebird

9A Crossley Regis

9B Daimler Royal Double-Six

9C Ford Popular

9D Ford Popular

9A: **Crossley** offered five models in chassis and saloon form, all featuring pre-selective four-speed gearbox. Regis models had 9 ft 0½ in wheelbase, 2- and 3-Litre models 10 ft 2½ in. The Regis Sports Saloon shown had a 35½-bhp 1122-cc (63×90 mm) engine with overhead and side valves.

9B: **Daimler** Royal Double-Six, one of several state cars used by King George V. The complete Daimler range for 1935 comprised five 15 HP models (45-bhp 2003-cc Six, wb 9 ft 1½ in, £450–£475), three 20 HP models (59-bhp 2687-cc Six, wb 10 ft 4 in, £695–£795), two 25 HP Straight Eight models (89-bhp 3746-cc Eight, wb 11 ft 10 in, £1495–£1515), one 40 HP chassis (105-bhp 5296-cc V12, wb 12 ft 3½ in) and one 50 HP chassis (132-bhp 6511-cc V12, wb 12 ft 3½ in). The last two had sleeve-valve engines; all others had pushrod-operated overhead valves. All models had Fluid Flywheel with pre-selective four-speed gearbox.

9C: **Ford** Popular 8 HP (Model Y) was continued in chassis, Tudor, Fordor and 5-cwt Van form. Picture shows a Tudor, or Single-Entrance Saloon, negotiating a flooded road at Owston Ferry in Yorkshire.

9D: **Ford** Popular chassis was available for £97 10s. for coachbuilt bodywork, exemplified by this neat little Drophead Coupé.

## 1935

10A: **Ford** De Luxe 10 HP Model C was new stablemate for the Popular. It had the same 7 ft 6 in wheelbase but was roomier, more luxurious and powered by a new 1172-cc (63·5 × 92·5 mm) 10 HP 32·5-bhp side-valve engine, which was basically a larger-bore version of the Popular's 933-cc (56·6 × 92·5 mm) 7·96 HP 22-bhp unit. Within the Ford organization the Model C De Luxe was known also by the designation 20E, the Model Y Popular as 19E. Picture shows touring model in South Africa, after class win in the 1935 Capetown-Port Elizabeth-Capetown reliability trial.

10A Ford De Luxe

10C Ford V8

10B: **Ford** V8 was available in Britain with two types of engine. The model 48 was similar in all but minor details to the North American 1935 Ford, powered by the 30 HP 90-bhp 3622-cc (77·79 × 95·25 mm) side-valve V-8-cylinder engine. The Model 60, which was externally similar to the Model 48, had the smaller 22 HP 2227-cc (66·04 × 81·28 mm) variant, resulting in a road tax reduction from £22 10s. to £16 10s. The Model 60 was produced in Britain until 1936 when it was replaced by a new 22 HP with European style bodywork.

10C: **Ford** V8 chassis was available for special bodywork and sold at £190 (October 1935). These three illustrations show some special versions offered by Dagenham Motors Limited, viz. DM Sports Saloon (top; price £425) and a Foursome Drophead Coupé (£415) with the top in closed and half-open position.

10D: **Ford** V8 chassis was very suitable for newspaper delivery. Shown is one of two vans operated by The Star. The bodywork was by G. Scammell and Nephew Limited of London. Doors and front roof section were from the Standard Saloon.

10B Ford V8

10D Ford

11A: **Frazer-Nash** TT (1934) Replica was offered with four- or six-cylinder engine. The Four had a 1496-cc (69 x 100 mm) single-OHC power unit, rated at 11·9 HP and a four-speed gearbox. Final drive to the solid rear axle was by chain. It cost £650.

11B: **Hillman** Minx range, Rootes' 'bread and butter line', was modified in various details for 1935. It was a very popular car and good value. Features included (quoting from the sales literature): 'roomy comfort; draughtless ventilation; synchromesh gear-change; modernistic, sane beauty; cushioned power; cyclonic induction.' It retained the 1185-cc (63 x 95 mm) 27-bhp side-valve engine, rated at 9·8 HP. 1935 models had a new radiator grille/shell and the filler cap under the bonnet.

11C: **Hillman** Minx Family Saloon sold at £159. A radio-equipped variant, called the Melody Minx, cost £195.

11D: **Hillman** Aero Minx Cresta Saloon was a new model on the Aero Minx Safe Speed chassis. It costs £265 and the engine developed ten more brake horsepower than the standard Minx. The Cresta, Hillman proclaimed, was 'not only nippy but definitely natty'.

11E: **Hillman** Aero Minx Two-seater. This smart little sports car was offered at a mere £225. Wheelbase of the Aero Minxes was four inches shorter than the standard models, at 7 ft 4 in. Shown in the car at the Olympia Motor Show is actress Nell Gwyn, wearing the costume used in a recent successful film.

11A Frazer-Nash TT Replica

11B Hillman Minx

11C Hillman Minx

11D Hillman Aero Minx

11E Hillman Aero Minx

## 1935

12A Hillman Twenty-70

12B : Hillman Twenty-70

12C Hillman Twenty-70

12A : **Hillman** Twenty-70 Saloon, one of a large fleet supplied to the Iranian Oil Company for service in South Persia. The order also included a number of pickup trucks on the same chassis. Non-standard wheels and tyres were specified.
12B : **Hillman** Twenty-70 with Wingham Cabriolet four-seater body was offered at £395. The Twenty-70 models had a 20·9 HP 68-bhp side-valve Six engine of 2810-cc capacity. There was also the Sixteen which was similar in specification but had a 15·9 HP 50-bhp 2110-cc engine (65- instead of 75-mm bore).
12C : **Hillman** Twenty-70 LWB Tourers supplied for Trans-Jordan Frontier Force. Bodywork was by Maidstone. LWB models had 10 ft 3 in wheelbase instead of 9 ft 3 in.
12D : **Hillman** Twenty-70 as assembled in Sydney, Australia. These cars differed from the British parent vehicle in various bodywork details. Note horizontal bonnet louvres.

12D Hillman Twenty-70

13A: **Humber** Twelve was virtually a new car for the 1935 selling season. It was also known as the Twelve-45 and was available as Saloon (£285), Vogue Saloon (two-door, £335) and Foursome Drophead Coupé (shown, £325). Wheelbase was 8 ft $2\frac{3}{4}$ in. The cars were powered by a 1669-cc (69·5×110 mm) 42-bhp side-valve Four, rated at 11·98 HP. All four forward speeds had synchromesh.
13B: **Humber** Twelve Saloon. All Twelves had a new chassis frame and the engine and radiator were mounted several inches farther forward than before. Tyre size was 5·50-17.
13C: **Humber** 16/60 Six-light Saloon, costing £435. The 16/60, the Snipe 80 and the Pullman followed similar general lines, most constructional features being common to all. The 16/60 had 10 ft 4 in wheelbase chassis and bodywork similar to the Snipe 80 but its 16·9 HP six-cylinder engine was of 2276-cc capacity (67·5×106 mm) and developed 55 bhp at 3600 rpm. The tyre size was 6·00-18.

13B Humber Twelve

13A Humber Twelve

13C Humber 16/60

## 1935

14A: **Humber** Snipe 80 Sports Saloon, selling at £550, was one of five factory-built body styles available. The engine was a 23·8 HP side-valve Six of 3498·5-cc capacity (80 × 116 mm), developing 77 bhp at 3400 rpm. Tyres were 6·50-17.
14B: **Humber** Pullman shared $3\frac{1}{2}$-litre 77-bhp engine with Snipe 80 but had 11 ft wheelbase and 7·00-18 tyres. The Pullman Sedanca De Ville shown was priced at £945 and owned by Mr and Mrs Sonny Hale, the latter of course being the famous Jessie Matthews.
14C: **Humber** Pullman Landaulette. Humber Pullmans were frequently used by Royalty, including the late Duke of Windsor (shown).

14B Humber Pullman

14A Humber Snipe 80

14C Humber Pullman

15A Jensen/Ford

15B Jensen/Ford

15A-B: **Jensen/Ford** constituted an American (Canadian) Ford V8 30 HP chassis with numerous modifications carried out by Jensens of West Bromwich. The chassis was lowered and the radiator dropped to reduce overall height. This very rare shooting brake was rescued from a farm in Surrey and is shown as found, awaiting restoration.
15C: **Jowett** 5G Long two-seater with dicky seat, also known as Flying Fox. All Jowett models were powered by a 16-bhp 907-cc (75·4 × 101·6 mm) water-cooled flat-twin engine with side valves, rated at 7·04 HP.
15D: **Lagonda** Rapier 10 HP, available only in chassis form, was smallest and cheapest Lagonda offered during 1934-35. It had an 8 ft 4 in wheelbase and cost £270. The four-cylinder twin-OHC 1104-cc engine produced 45 bhp at 4500 rpm. Shown is a surviving Pillarless Saloon by Eagle, one of only two built.
15E: **Lagonda** Rapier chassis was used chiefly for sports type cars. The production run of this attractive Two-seater by Eagle, another survivor, remained under twelve.

15D Lagonda Rapier

15E Lagonda Rapier

15C Jowett 5G Long

## 1935

16A: **Lagonda** 4½-Litre models came in two versions, the basic Six with 10 ft 9 in wheelbase and 104-bhp engine and the Rapide with 10 ft 3 in wheelbase and 120-bhp engine. Both engines were 29·13 HP six-cylinder OHV units with 88·5-mm bore but the stroke of the Rapide engine was 120·6 vs. 120 mm, resulting in a cubic capacity of 4467 cc. Lagonda also offered smaller six-cylinder models, down to the 16/80 Special with 1991-cc engine.
16B: **Lanchester** 18 was basically a Daimler (Lanchester had been taken over in 1931 by the BSA Group of which Daimler had been a member since 1910). The 18 had a 53-bhp 2390-cc six-cylinder OHV engine with fixed cylinder head. Transmission comprised Daimler Fluid Flywheel with self-changing gearbox.

16C-D: **MG** P-Series was developed from the J-Series and had a sturdier chassis, better brakes, three-bearing crankshaft and other refinements. The PB-type Midget of 1935/36 was available in Two-seater (shown), Four-seater and Airline Coupé variants and had a 939-cc (60 × 83 mm) four-cylinder engine, developing 43 bhp at 5500 rpm. Its immediate predecessor, the 1934 PA Midget had a 36-bhp 847-cc (57 × 83 mm) engine. Both engines had overhead camshaft, twin SU carburettors and four-speed gearbox. The PB had a slatted radiator grille instead of plain as on the PA. Some 2500 of the P-Series were produced.

16A Lagonda 4½-Litre

16B Lanchester 18

16C MG Midget

16D MG Midget

17A : **MG** NA Magnette Four-seater was one of several models available in the six-cylinder N-Series. It had a 1286-cc OHC engine with twin SU carburettors, developing 56 bhp at 5500 rpm, and four-speed gearbox.
17B : **Morgan** Family Model was claimed to offer 'the cheapest form of comfortable motoring for more than one person'. It was a four-seater three-wheeler with V-twin side-valve water-cooled engine. Road tax was only £4 per year, and the car cost £105 (£96 12s. in 1936).
17C : **Morris** Eight Tourers were used in some quantity by the British Army as signals cars. In June, 1935, the Eight was designated Series I. They retained the 22·5-bhp 918-cc (57 × 90 mm) side-valve engine and three-speed gearbox. Note the military cross-country-type tyres and the radiator muff.
17D : **Morris/Jensen** Eight Sports Tourer. This was one of about one hundred cars with special bodywork by Jensen Motors Limited of West Bromwich. As Michael Sedgwick put it : 'Jensen's idea of a Series I sports four-seater was pleasing but it was also a lot more expensive than the standard model, and lacked the latter's elegant simplicity'. The standard model cost £120, the Jensen £165.
17E : **Morris** Eight 5-cwt Van was popular for delivery work in towns and rural areas.

17A MG Magnette

17C Morris Eight

17D Morris/Jensen Eight

17B Morgan Three-Wheeler

17E Morris Eight

18A: **Morris** Ten-Four Saloon was available with Sliding-head at £175 and with Fixed-head at £169 10s. The 10 HP 1292-cc (63·5 × 102 mm) four-cylinder side-valve engine developed 26·5 bhp. Except for the Eight all Morrises had four-speed gearboxes.
18B: **Morris** Twelve-Four (formerly Cowley Four) was available in chassis form at £130 and formed an ideal basis for a medium capacity delivery van. This model had an 8 ft 6 in wheelbase and 5·00-19 tyres. Engine was 11·9 HP side-valve Four of 1550-cc capacity (69·5 × 102 mm). Saloons were available on this chassis with or without sliding roof.

18A Morris Ten-Four

18B Morris Twelve-Four

18C Morris Oxford Sixteen

18D Riley 1½-Litre Lynx

18C: **Morris** Oxford Sixteen had six-cylinder side-valve engine, four-speed synchromesh gearbox with Bendix automatic clutch control, 9 ft 6 in wheelbase and 5·50-17 tyres. Saloon (shown) and Special Coupé body styles were available, costing £285 and £305 respectively. There was a choice of engines: 2062-cc (65·5 × 102 mm, 39 bhp) or 2561-cc (73 × 102 mm, 52 bhp). The latter was known as the Oxford Twenty.
18D: **Riley** 1½-Litre 12 HP Series was new for 1935 and comprised Falcon and Kestrel Saloons and the smart Lynx Open Tourer. The engine was a 46-bhp pushrod OHV Four with a cubic capacity of 1496 cc (69 × 100 mm) and a treasury rating of 11·81 HP. The Lynx shown has survived in Cheshire and is the earliest still in existence.

19A: **Riley** Kestrel Saloon body style was produced during 1932-39. It featured a sharply sloping tail ('fastback') with the typical Riley style side windows and was available on several of the company's four- and six-cylinder chassis.
19B: **Rolls-Royce** 20/25 Saloon Landaulette supplied by Dorking Motor Co Ltd in 1935. The 20/25 chassis, costing £1050, had a wheelbase of 11 ft and was used by several coachbuilders. The engine was a 3669-cc (82×114 mm) six-cylinder, rated at 25·3 HP, with seven-bearing crankshaft.
19C: **Rover** 1935 programme comprised 10, 12 and 14 HP models, as well as Speed Fourteen and Speed Twenty Sports type cars. Prices ranged from £248 up to £495.
19D: **Rover** Twelve was available in Saloon, Sports Saloon (shown) and Open Four-seater form. The latter two were built on an 8 ft 9 in chassis (like the Rover Ten), the Saloon on 9 ft 4 in. The Twelve chassis was available, at £195, with either wheelbase size. Engine was a $1\frac{1}{2}$-litre OHV Four, rated at 11·9 HP but developing 48 bhp at 4200 rpm. Gearbox was four-speed with freewheel.

19A Riley Kestrel

19C Rover 10-14 HP

19B Rolls-Royce 20/25

19D Rover Twelve

20A: **Rytecraft** Scootacar was the name of the petrol-engined development of an electric 'dodgem' car, produced by the British Motor Boat Mfg Co Ltd in London during 1934-40. This 1935 model, powered by a 98-cc Villiers Midget industrial engine, was driven round the world in 1965/66 by its enterprising owner Mr Jim Parkinson, shown here at a Redhill, Surrey, school fête after his return.

20B: **Singer** offered a wide range of models on their Nine, Eleven, $1\frac{1}{2}$-litre, Fourteen and Sixteen chassis. Shown is an Eleven Saloon, crossing Conway Bridge during the Welsh Rally, 1935.

20C: **Singer** Eleven Drop-head Coupé, price £275. The Eleven featured independent front suspension (as did certain Nine models) and had Fluidrive transmission. Engine was a 10·5 HP OHC Four of 1384-cc (65 × 105 mm) capacity, developing 35 bhp. Wheelbase was 8 ft 4 in.

20D: **Singer** Eleven Airstream Saloon was carry-over from the previous model year. Price was £300. It was not continued for 1936. Like the other Elevens it had independent front suspension and Fluidrive transmission with freewheel and clutch-less gear change.

20A Rytecraft Scootacar

20C Singer Eleven

20B Singer Eleven

20D Singer Eleven Airstream

21A: **Singer** Nine Le Mans Two-seater at Brooklands. The Le Mans models had basically the same 972-cc engine as the standard Nines but with twin carbs, developing 34 bhp (Speed model 38 bhp). The Two-seater cost £215.
21B: **Singer** Nine Le Mans Replica (No. 49) negotiating 'Les Esses' at Le Mans. No. 12 is an Alfa-Romeo.
21C: **SS** 90 was a 90-mph two-seater sports car and appeared in March, 1935. It had a 2663·7-cc (73 × 106 mm) six-cylinder side-valve engine. Power output was 68 bhp at 3600 rpm. At the rear there was a slab-mounted fuel tank and a vertically mounted spare wheel. This car was the immediate predecessor of the famed SS Jaguar 100.
21D: **SS** I Airline Saloon was available with 53-bhp 2143-cc (65·5 × 106 mm) 15·96 HP engine or with 68-bhp 2663·7-cc (73 × 106 mm) 19·84 HP variant. Both were side-valve six-cylinders. Wheelbase was 9 ft 11 in for both types. Saloon and Tourer bodystyles were available on the same chassis, as well as on 8 ft 8 in wheelbase four-cylinder 10 and 12 HP SS II variants.

21A Singer Nine Le Mans

21B Singer Nine Le Mans

21C SS 90

21D SS I Airline

# 1935

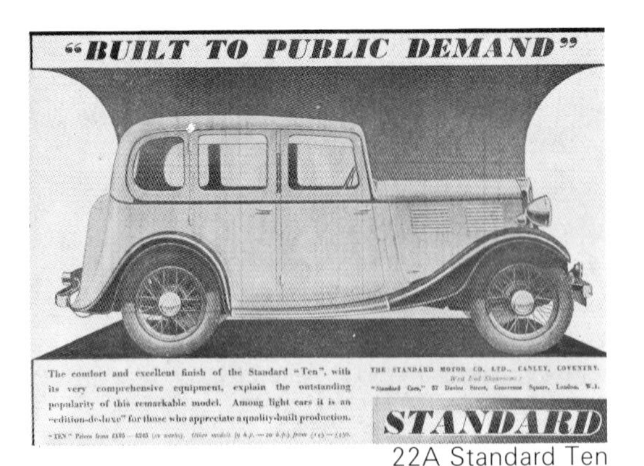


22A Standard Ten

22B Sunbeam

22C Sunbeam Twenty-Five

22A: **Standard** Ten had 1343-cc (63·5 × 106 mm) four-cylinder engine, rated at 10 HP, and 7 ft 10 in wheelbase. There was also a Ten-Twelve Speed Saloon variant with twin-carburettor high-compression 12 HP engine.

22B: **Sunbeam** offered 12·8 HP Four and 19·8, 20·9 and 23·8 HP Six models. This six-cylinder example was still operational in Devon in the late 1960s.

22C: **Sunbeam** Twenty-Five (23·8 HP) Limousine, acquired by HRH The Duke of Gloucester in March, 1935. It had a 3317·5-cc (80 × 100 mm) OHV six-cylinder engine and 11 ft 4 in wheelbase. SWB Twenty-Fives (10 ft 10 in) were easily distinguishable by not having the headlamp tie bar in front of the radiator.

22D: **Talbot** Seventy-Five Special Drop-frame Sports Saloon (Model BA75) was one of three saloons available. It cost £565 and had a 17·9 HP 70-bhp six-cylinder OHV engine of 2276-cc capacity (69·5 × 100 mm). The transmission was of the automatic four-speed pre-selecting type.

22E: **Triumph** model range comprised Gloria Fours and Sixes, all with Coventry Climax engines with overhead inlet and side exhaust valves. The cheapest model was the 10·8 HP Gloria Four Southern Cross Two-seater, at £275. At the other end of the scale was the 15·72 HP Gloria Vitesse Six Flow-Free Saloon, priced at £425.

22D Talbot Seventy-Five

22E Triumph Gloria

23A: **Triumph** Gloria Vitesse Six Flow-Free Saloon had very smart appearance. This body was mounted only on the Vitesse chassis which had a specially tuned engine, developing 65 bhp. All Triumphs featured a free-wheel and remote control gear selection, as well as Lucas Startix ignition systems. Twin fuel tanks were located in the rear wings.
23B: **Vauxhall** Light Six D-Series, launched in late 1934, comprised DY 12 HP and DX 14 HP models. They superseded the 1933-34 A-series and featured independent front wheel suspension. Prices for 12 and 14 HP were the same: chassis £150, Saloon (12 HP only) £205, Saloon De Luxe £225. The 1531-cc (57 x 100 mm) and 1781-cc (61·5 x 100 mm) OHV engines had an output of 36 and 42 bhp respectively.
23C: **Vauxhall** Light Six DY and DX chassis were available at £150 for special coachwork such as this four-seater Coupé.
23D: **Vauxhall** Big Six B-series was available with 19·8 HP 2392-cc (73 x 95·25 mm) or 26·3 HP 3180-cc (84·14 x 95·25 mm) OHV Six engine. These models were designated BY and BX respectively. Standard wheelbase was 9 ft 3 in but a long-wheelbase version, Model BXL, was available with the 26·3 HP engine. With seven-seater Limousine bodywork the BXL sold at £550. This wartime Salvation Army mobile canteen, paid for by the inhabitants of Wellesley, Massachusetts, USA, through the British War Relief Society, was a 1939/40 conversion of the standard-wheelbase Saloon.
23E: **Wolseley** offered a wide range of cars from 8·95 up to 20·93 HP. Shown in this period advertisement are some of the models offered by the London Distributors.

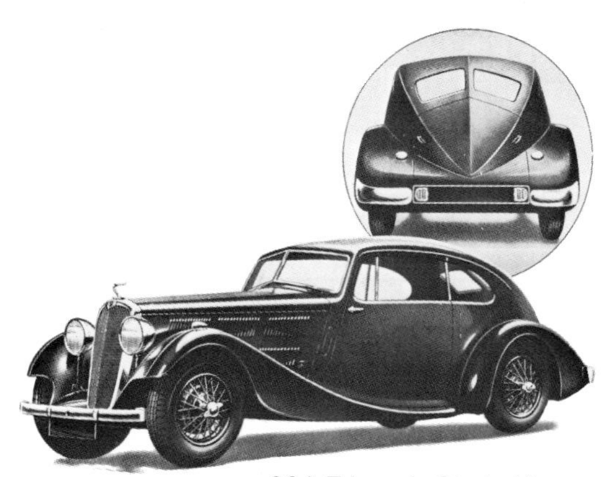

23A Triumph Gloria Vitesse

23B Vauxhall Light Six

23C Vauxhall Light Six

23D Vauxhall Big Six

23E Wolseley 14 HP

**1936** In September 1936 there were nearly $2\frac{1}{4}$ million motor vehicles of all types registered in the United Kingdom, including 1,762,924 cars (87,820 of which were registered as hackney carriages) and 467,561 trucks and buses. There was now one car per 21 inhabitants, which placed Great Britain in fifth position internationally in terms of 'car density'. Production statistics for the 1936 calendar year showed figures of 367,237 cars and 114,305 commercials, giving a total of 481,542 new vehicles for home and export sales. Exports reached a new record with overseas sales valued at over £10 million for the first time. This represented 64,765 cars and 17,571 commercials, including chassis.

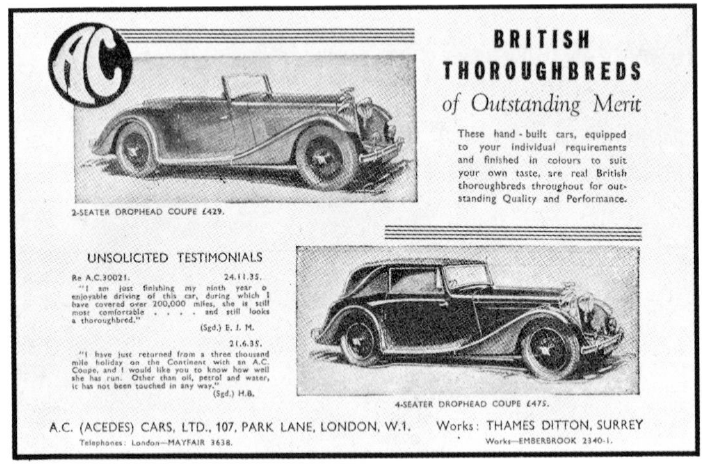

24A AC Ace

24B AC Ace 16/60

24C Alvis $3\frac{1}{2}$-Litre

24A: **AC** Ace models all had the well-proven 1991-cc (65 × 100 mm) OHC engine, rated at 15·7 HP. Actual bhp figures were 56 for the 16/56, 66 for the 16/66 and 80 for the 16/80.
24B: **AC** Ace 16/60 Family Saloon had Sunshine roof as standard equipment and cost £485. Wheelbase was 9 ft 7 in. Overall length was 14 ft 10 in. All models had 5·00-19 tyres on wire wheels.
24C: **Alvis** 1936 programme comprised Firebird, Silver Eagle Sixteen, Crested Eagle and Speed Twenty models, all available in chassis form or with factory supplied bodywork. Prices of complete cars ranged from £490 up to £900. In addition there was the $3\frac{1}{2}$-Litre, available only in chassis form. One of these is shown here, with Sedanca De Ville coachwork by Mayfair. It had a three-carburettor 102-bhp OHV engine of 3571-cc (83 × 110 mm) capacity. Like the Crested Eagle and the Speed Twenty it had independent front suspension with a transverse leaf spring.

Imports amounted to 12,143 and 2,700 units respectively, worth almost £2.5 million. New vehicle registrations during 1936 totalled 471,914. The majority of these, namely 310,091, were private cars. 8,212 new 'hackneys' were registered.

---

25A Armstrong Siddeley Twelve-Plus

25B Aston-Martin Two-Litre

25A: **Armstrong Siddeley** offered 12, 14, 17 and 20 HP models, priced from £285 up to £745. Shown in this period advertisement is the Twelve-Plus (14 HP) Saloon De Luxe, a new model, priced at £320. All models had six-cylinder engines with overhead valves except the 12 HP which had side valves. The 12, 17 and 20 HP were carryovers from 1935, with detail improvements.
25B: **Aston-Martin** Two-Litre Four, belonging to Eddy Herzbergen. This car took part in the Mille Miglia and is photographed here with Mr Piet Olyslager (left) and Jacques van der Peil, at Zeist, Netherlands, in the Spring of 1937.
25C: **Austin** Twelve-Four Ascot De Luxe Saloon cost £208 and had sunshine roof and leather upholstery as standard equipment (unlike the £188 fixed-head model). Engine was a 28-bhp 1535-cc side-valve Four, rated at 11·9 HP.
25D: **Austin** Seven Ruby Saloon, Model ARQ. The Seven was continued from 1935 with only detail modifications.

25C Austin Twelve-Four

25D Austin Seven

26A Austin Twenty

26B Bentley 3½-Litre

26C Chrysler Wimbledon

26A: **Austin** Twenty Mayfair Landaulet. This was Austin's largest car, with 11 ft 4 in wheelbase and 57·5-bhp 3·4-litre six-cylinder engine, rated at 23·5 HP. It featured Girling brakes and Jackall hydraulic jacks. The 'easy-clean' wheels were standard for the 1937 model year.
26B: **Bentley** 3½-Litre cost £1100 in chassis form and special coachwork was built on it by several firms. This 'razor-edge' four-light saloon is a good example. Complete cars available from Bentley Motors were an Open Tourer (£1380), a Four-door Saloon (£1460) and a Drophead Coupé (£1485).
26C: **Chrysler** Motors Ltd of Mortlake Road, Kew Gardens, Surrey, offered a variety of assembled American Plymouth and Chrysler Six and Eight models, all under the Chrysler name. Shown is a Chrysler Wimbledon Six which had a 23·4 HP 82-bhp L-head Six engine. Basically it was a luxury edition of the Plymouth P2. The basic P2 was offered as Chrysler Kew, with 19·8 HP export engine as standard equipment.
26D: **Crossley** Regis 1½-Litre Saloon cost £365 and was first introduced in 1935. The 1476-cc six-cylinder engine was rated at 12·9 HP.

26D Crossley Regis

27A Daimler Straight Eight

27B Ford Popular

27C Ford De Luxe

27A: **Daimler** 31·74 HP Straight Eight chassis with Hooper coachwork. The chassis cost £900 and had a wheelbase of 11 ft 10 in. Wire spoke wheels were standard and the tyre size was 7·00-18. The 12-cylinder Double Six 50 chassis had a wheelbase of 13 ft 1 in and cost £1650.
27B: **Ford** Popular Saloon, Model Y, with 7·96 HP engine was available with two- and four-door bodywork, known as the single- and double-entrance model respectively. The former's price had been reduced to £100 and it became generally known as the '£100 Ford'. To achieve this low price Ford had simplified the car's specification which was now rather austere, but, as this illustration suggests, it was more comfortable than waiting at the bus stop!
27C: **Ford** De Luxe, Model C, was available as two- or four-door Saloon or with Touring body as shown here. The Model C, which had a 10 HP 32·5-bhp 1172-cc L-head Four engine, differed from the 1935 model mainly in having three horizontal chrome strips on the radiator grille and vertical bonnet louvres, also with three chrome strips. Prices: Chassis £110, Two-door Saloon and Touring £135, Four-door (Double-Entrance) Saloon £145.
27D: **Ford** V8, Model 60, with 22 HP (63-bhp) engine was carryover from 1935 (when it was also available as Model 48 with 30 HP engine). Later in the season it was replaced by the Model 62 (*q.v.*). It is shown here with the smaller De Luxe Model C in order to show the similarity of the two designs.

27D Ford De Luxe and V8

28A Ford V8 Model 62

28B Ford V8 Model 68

28C Frazer-Nash Ulster 100

28A: **Ford** V8, Model 62, superseded the 1935 American-style Model 60 in 1936 (for the 1937 model year) and was entirely British-made. It was, however, unmistakably a Ford and other European Ford plants, namely in France and Germany, produced very similar 'small V8s'. The engine was a 22 HP of 2226·9-cc (66·04 × 81·28 mm) capacity, developing 63 bhp at 4300 rpm. The wheelbase was 9 ft $0\frac{1}{4}$ in. Transmission, chassis, suspension, etc. were similar to that of the American Ford. Both had 6·00-16 tyres. The new saloon was priced at £210. There were no alternative body styles.
28B: **Ford** V8, Model 68 Fordor Saloon with 30 HP engine. This, the 'real Ford V8', was virtually the same as the North American Model 68. It had the 3621·5-cc (77·78 × 95·25 mm) V-8-cylinder engine, developing 88·5 bhp at 3700 rpm and rated at 30·01 HP. It had, of course, right-hand drive. Wheelbase was 9 ft 4 in.
28C: **Frazer-Nash** Ulster 100 was one of several sports and racing cars produced by AFN Ltd of Isleworth, Middlesex. The Ulster 100 was, in effect, a modified edition of their TT Replica model, with a new streamlined body, and cost £625–£650, depending on engine type. The spare wheel was mounted vertically and lengthwise in the pointed tail section. Engine was a 1496-cc (69 × 100 mm) OHV or OHC four-cylinder, rated at 11·9 HP. Later a twin-OHC version became optional. AFN also offered a range of six-cylinder $1\frac{1}{2}$- and 2- litre BMW-based models, priced from £298 up to £460.
28D-E: **Hillman** Minx was entirely restyled but retained the well-proven 9·8 HP 1185-cc side-valve Four engine. The main body shell, with the later addition of a built-in boot, was to continue until after the 1939-45 war. 1936 Minx buyers had the option of a folding luggage grid which cost £2 7s. 6d, painted. The Minx Saloon retained its £159 price tag; the De Luxe model (with sun roof as shown) was reduced in price, to £175.

28D Hillman Minx

28E Hillman Minx

29A Hillman Minx

29A: **Hillman** Minx Four-door Tourer in India. In the UK this model sold at £175 or, with De Luxe trim, £190. Also available was a Foursome Coupé (convertible), at £215.

29B: **Hillman** Hawk Saloon, photographed at Lynton, North Devon. The Hawk was a new model, powered by a six-cylinder 3181-cc (75 × 120 mm) side-valve engine, developing 75-bhp at 3400 rpm and rated at 20·92 HP. It had a 9 ft 0½ in wheelbase and was available also as Sixteen with 16·95 HP 56-bhp 2576-cc (67·5 × 120 mm) power unit. Tyre size was 6·50-16. All six-cylinder Hillmans had Evenkeel IFS with transverse leaf spring.

29C: **Hillman** Hawk Tourer, one of a batch supplied to the War Office. Bodywork was by Coachcraft (shown) and Mulliners.

29D: **Hillman** 80 was generally similar to the Hawk but had 10 ft 6 in wheelbase. Shown is a Limousine with oversize tyres, one of a fleet of Hawks and 80s supplied to the Anglo-Iranian Oil Company for use in Persia.

29B Hillman Hawk

29C Hillman Hawk

29D Hillman 80

## 1936

30A: **Hillman** 80 Touring Car as supplied to the Trans-Jordan Frontier Force. These cars were equipped with spare water and petrol tanks (visible in rear compartment) thus permitting operation at long distances from base. Spare road springs were carried at front and rear, doubling up as bumpers.
30B: **Humber** Twelve for 1936 featured minor styling changes. The Six-Light Saloon shown sold for £285. Engine was 1669-cc (69 × 110 mm) side-valve Four.
30C: **Humber** Twelve Vogue Two-door pillarless Saloon. Picture shows side-opening lid of built-in luggage boot.

---

30A Hillman 80

30B Humber Twelve

30C Humber Twelve

31A: **Humber** Eighteen, small-bore edition of the Snipe, at Olympia. The Eighteen superseded the 16/60 of previous years. Bore and stroke were 69·5 × 120 mm, giving a cubic capacity of 2731 cc and an HP rating of 17·97. Brake horsepower was 65 at 3600 rpm. All six-cylinder Humbers now had independent front suspension and the cars were becoming increasingly similar to comparable Hillman models, both manufacturers being divisions of the Rootes Group. Eighteen and Snipe were available with four factory-supplied body styles; the former were £30 cheaper throughout the range.
31B: **Humber** Snipe Six-light Saloon, priced at £475. The Snipe had the same 120-mm stroke as the Eighteen but an 85-mm bore. Cubic capacity was 4086 cc, output 100 bhp at 3400 rpm and treasury rating 26·88 HP. Wheelbase for both was 10 ft 4 in, tyre size 7·50-16.
31C: **Humber** Snipe Sports Saloon, selling for £550, featuring large built-in boot and spare wheel with cover.
31D: **Humber** Pullman was similar in most respects to the Snipe but the wheelbase was longer, at 11 ft $0\frac{1}{4}$ in. Prices were £425 for the chassis, £735 for the Limousine and Landaulette, £895 for the Sedanca Coupé and £975 for the Sedanca De Ville. Picture shows HM King Edward VIII (the late Duke of Windsor) in back of car, at Vimy Ridge, France, after the unveiling of the Canadian War Memorial on 26 July, 1936.

31B Humber Snipe

31C Humber Snipe

31A Humber Eighteen

31D Humber Pullman

32A: **Jowett** offered two model ranges, namely the 6G Series with the 7 HP 907-cc (75·4 × 101·6 mm) 16-bhp flat-twin engine and the J Series with a new 10 HP 1166-cc (63·5 × 92 mm) 31-bhp flat-four. Both had 8 ft 6 in wheelbase. The 10 HP (centre) Saloon was offered as Jupiter (£197 10s.) and Jason (£215), the 7 HP was available with four body styles.

32B-C: **Lagonda** Rapier chassis production was discontinued and the production rights were sold to Rapier Cars Ltd of Hammersmith Road, London W6, who, under designer Ashcroft, continued to manufacture Rapiers in modest numbers until 1939. The Drophead Coupé (32B), which has survived, is one of only nine known to have been built. The Two-seater (32C), seen in the late sixties, is the only one known to have existed.

32D: **Lagonda** Tourer was one of three factory-supplied body styles on the firm's £795 4½-litre chassis. It cost exactly £1000. The others were a Four-door Saloon at £1085 and a Drophead Coupé at £1125. The six-cylinder engine, rated at 29·13 HP, developed 140 bhp and had twin SU carburettors. Wheelbase was 10 ft 9 in, tyre size 6·00-18.

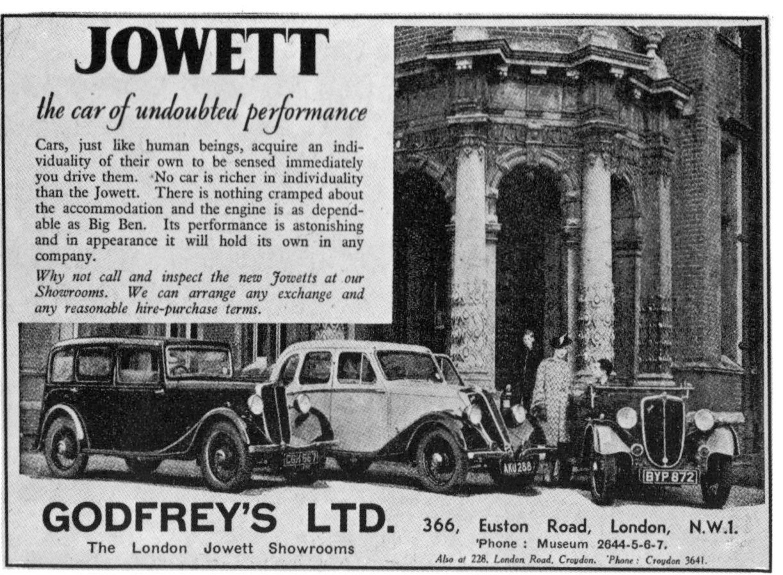


32A Jowett 6G and J Series

32B Lagonda Rapier

32C Lagonda Rapier

32D Lagonda

33A Lanchester 10

33B Lanchester Straight Eight

33A: **Lanchester** 10 Saloon was one of five body types offered (£298-£325), in addition to the chassis which was available for £215. Engine was a 1444-cc OHV Four, coupled to Daimler Fluid Flywheel transmission.
33B: **Lanchester** Straight Eight with Hooper Landaulette coachwork for HRH the Duke of York (later King George VI). The chassis was, in fact, that of the then-new Daimler Straight Eight (*q.v.*), only a few of which were used in Lanchester guise for special customers of the *marque*.

33C: **MG** T-Series Midget TA was introduced in 1936 and developed from the 1935 PB-type. Compared with the PB it was larger and had a 10 HP 1292-cc (63·5 × 102 mm) OHV four-cylinder engine, developing 50 bhp at 4000 rpm. Two-seater version is shown.
33D: **MG** SA-Series Two-Litre was available with Saloon, Tourer and Convertible (shown) bodywork or as a bare chassis at £250. The six-cylinder OHV engine was of 2288-cc capacity (69 × 102 mm), developing 78·5 bhp at 4200 rpm.

33C MG Midget

33D MG Two-Litre

34A: **MG** SA-Series Two-Litre chassis had a long wheelbase (10 ft 3 in) and 5·50-18 tyres on centre-lock wire wheels.
34B: **Morgan** Model F Two-seater could be supplied with either 933-cc or 1172-cc side-valve four-cylinder engine (Ford 8 HP and 10 HP resp.). It had a maximum speed of over 65 mph and would cruise at 60. Final drive was by single chain from worm drive sprocket.
34C: **Morris** range comprised Series I Eight and Series II Ten, Twelve, Sixteen, Eighteen, Twenty-One and Twenty-Five HP models. From the Sixteen upwards all had six cylinders, the smaller ones had four. All were side-valve engines. Morris Motors emphasised 'Specialisation', which meant that they operated several separate factories each specializing in the manufacture of certain components, the SU Carburettor Co being a good example.
34D: **Railton** Carrington Foursome Drophead Coupé was one of eight models offered by Railton Cars. It was priced at £845 and built on the LWB (129-in) chassis which itself cost £548. There was also a 122-in chassis, costing £100 less. They were based on American Hudson mechanical components, including the 4·2-litre straight-eight L-head engine. Performance of these cars was phenomenal. They were the work of the well-known World Land Speed Record car designer Reid Railton and virtually hand-built in the old Invicta factory, Fairmile Engineering Co, at Cobham in Surrey.

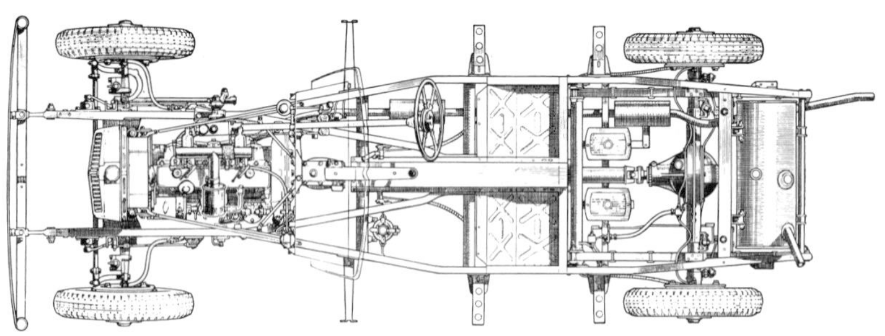

34A MG Two-Litre

34B Morgan Three-Wheeler

34C Morris Series II

34D Railton

# ADELPHI

The Adelphi is the finest all-purpose car the Riley Company has ever built. It is a full five-seater and its six-light coachbuilt body provides practically open car vision. Transmission is by Riley Pre-selectagear, the costliest and most satisfactory of all easy gear change systems. The Lever-free Front gives the driver the added advantages of "double entry," while true Inter-axle Seating and an air-liner braced box-section frame enables those high average speeds, of which all Riley cars are capable, to be enjoyed over the worst road surfaces. The 1½ Litre 12 h.p. Adelphi (Tax £9) costs £350. The 6 cyl. 15 h.p. Adelphi (Tax £11. 5. 0.) costs only £380. Dunlop Tyres and Triplex Glass all-round. Riley (Coventry) Limited, Coventry.

35A Riley Adelphi

35C Rover Twelve

35B Riley Lynx

35A: **Riley** Adelphi was a new five-seater body style, available on 1½-Litre, six-cylinder 15 HP and Eight-Ninety chassis.
35B: **Riley** Lynx four-door four-seater touring bodywork was available on 1½-Litre and six-cylinder 15 HP chassis, costing £345 and £375 respectively. There were also two 1½-Litre Special Series models, one selling for £372 and a Concours Model for £398; these had special engines with twin carburettors, two-port inlet manifolds, etc. Cheapest Riley was the Merlin Saloon on 9 HP chassis, at £269.
35C: **Rover** range comprised Ten, Twelve, Fourteen and Speed Fourteen models. Shown is a Twelve Saloon, which had an 11·9 HP OHV Four engine of 1495-cc capacity (69 × 100 mm). Power output was 48 bhp, wheelbase 9 ft 4 in.

36A SS Jaguar 100

36A: **SS** Jaguar 100 cost £395 and had 2½-litre six-cylinder OHV engine of 2663·7-cc capacity (73 x 106 mm) with twin carburettors, developing 104 bhp at 4500 rpm. A speed of 60 mph was easily reached in 12 seconds from standstill and the maximum speed was about 100 mph.

36B: **SS** Cars Ltd now used the name Jaguar, which was later to replace the name SS entirely. Shown is the six-cylinder OHV 2½-Litre Saloon, a slightly smaller edition of which was the 1½-Litre with side-valve Four. They cost £385 and £285 respectively.

36C: **Standard** introduced a new range of 'Flying' models with restyled bodywork. Shown is the Flying Twenty which had a 64-bhp side-valve engine of 2664-cc (73 x 106 mm) capacity, rated at 19·84 HP. Wheelbase was 9 ft 8 in, tyre size 5·50-17.

36B SS Jaguar 2½-Litre

36C Standard

## 1936

37A Sunbeam Thirty

37A: **Sunbeam** introduced a new model with a 4½-litre straight-eight engine, designed by George Roesch. Only four of these cars were made and all of them were probably dismantled. Shown is a catalogue picture of a Sedanca De Ville on the new Thirty chassis. It was priced at £1475. Sunbeam was part of the Sunbeam-Talbot-Darracq combine which was taken over by Rootes in 1935. The Sunbeam name was dropped and did not reappear until 1953, except on 1938-1954 Sunbeam-Talbots which were based on the later Rootes Talbots.
37B: **Talbot** Ten Sports Tourer was Hillman Minx-based car, conceived after the take-over of Clement-Talbot Ltd by Rootes. Picture shows the then well-known music hall comedians Clapham (left) and Dwyer at the Theatre Royal on the occasion of the former taking delivery of his new car.
37C: **Talbot** Ten Sports Saloon cost £265 and had pillarless bodywork. Engine was a 9·8 HP 1185-cc (63×95 mm) side-valve Four, similar to that of the Hillman Minx.
37D: **Talbot** range comprised Ten, 75, 105, 105 Speed, 3½-Litre and LWB models. Shown is a Six-light Saloon which was available on the 10 ft 0⅜ in wheelbase 75 and 105 chassis with 17·9 HP 2276-cc and 20·9 HP 2969-cc OHV Sixes respectively.

37B Talbot Ten

37C Talbot Ten

37D Talbot 75

38A Talbot 3½-Litre

38B Talbot 3½-Litre

38A: **Talbot** 3½-Litre Sports Tourer in Rootes' showroom in Devonshire House, Piccadilly, for many years the Rootes Group's headquarters. The 3½-Litre had a 23·8 HP 3377-cc (80 × 112 mm) OHV Six, developing 120 bhp at 4500 rpm.

38B: **Talbot** 3½-Litre Speed Sports Saloon cost £825 and featured graceful body styling. In a timed test at Brooklands it attained 92¾ mph and took just under 17 seconds to reach 60 mph from standstill.

38C: **Triumph** Gloria Six-cylinder Vitesse Tourer was typical of the company's sporty cars. The 1991-cc engine, designed by Coventry Climax, drove this 1½-ton handbuilt car at over 80 mph. The designation Vitesse indicated tuning modifications to give increased performance (65 bhp vs 55 bhp of standard Gloria Six).

38C Triumph Gloria Six Vitesse

39A Vauxhall Light Six

39C Wolseley 25 HP

39B Vauxhall 25 HP

39A: **Vauxhall** Light Six D-Series comprised 12 HP DY and 14 HP DX models which differed only in engine size. Both had six cylinders with 100-mm piston stroke but the bore was 57 mm for the 1·53-litre DY and 61·5 mm for the 1·78-litre DX.
39B: **Vauxhall** 25 HP G-Series was introduced in August 1936 and produced until 1939. There were two wheelbase lengths: Model GY with 9 ft $2\frac{1}{2}$ in for Saloon, Sports Saloon and Drophead Coupé and Model GL with 10 ft 10 in for Seven-Seater Saloon and Limousine. One of the latter is illustrated here. These cars had a 3215-cc (81·94 × 101·6 mm) OHV six-cylinder engine, giving a maximum speed of 80 mph. Standard equipment included a heater. 1936/37 models had a clutch-pedal-operated starter.
39C: **Wolseley** offered a wide range of models, varying from the £725 25 HP Limousine shown here down to the £165 Wasp Saloon. The 25 HP had an OHV six-cylinder engine of 3485-cc (82 × 110 mm) capacity. Wheelbase was 12 ft $1\frac{1}{4}$ in (10 ft $1\frac{1}{2}$ in for Saloon and Coupé), tyre size 7·00-16 (6·50-16).

**1937** During 1937 the British motor industry produced 379,310 cars and 113,946 commercial vehicles. Totalling almost half a million units this was a new record. During the same period a record 99,185 vehicles of all types were exported, valued at about £12¼ million, including £8,325,088 for 78,113 private cars and chassis. Total vehicle 'population' in the United Kingdom, according to the September Census, was nearing the 2½ million mark with 1,834,248 private cars, 87,474 'hackneys' and 487,750 commercials. Both production and exports, however, had reached a total which was not to be surpassed until after the second World War.
Imports were also highest of the decade, with 18,560 cars and 4,667 commercial vehicles, representing a total value of almost £3 million. New car registrations in 1937 amounted to 318,461.

40B Alta Sports

40A AC 16/60

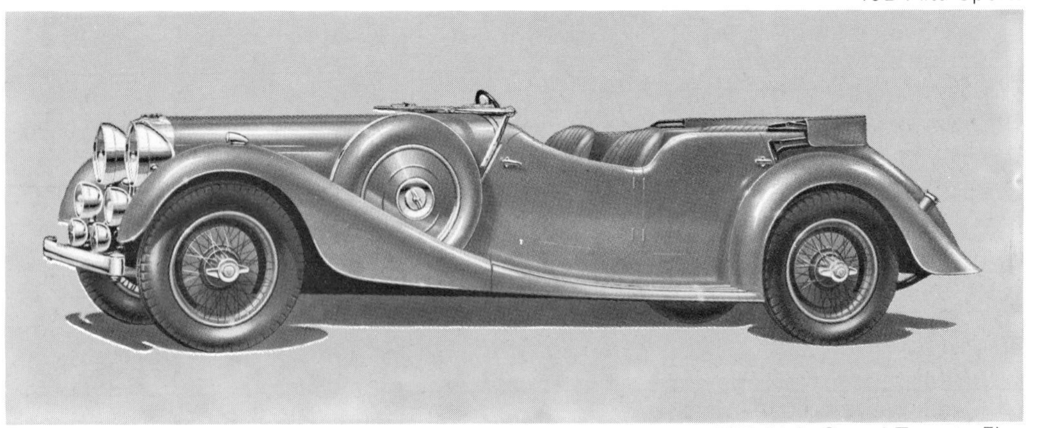

40C Alvis Speed Twenty Five

40A: **AC** 16/60 Fixed-head Coupé had 9 ft 7 in wheelbase and 5·50-18 tyres. The chassis cost £325. A 16/70 Sports chassis was available, with 5·50-19 tyres and 4·66 (vs. 4·5) to 1 final drive ratio, at £355. There was also a 16/80 Short Sports variant, at £365, with 8 ft 10 in wheelbase.
40B: **Alta** mainly produced racing cars (1100, 1½-litre, 2-litre and V8 models, priced from £850 up to £1750) but offered sports cars with any of the three four-cylinder engines used in the racing units. These were all equipped with an Alta-produced Roots type supercharger but the 1½- and 2-litre models were also available without this feature.
Bodywork shown was one of various types which could be supplied.
40C: **Alvis** Speed Twenty Five, shown with Cross and Ellis Four-seater Sports bodywork, had a six-cylinder 3571-cc OHV engine, rated at 25·63 HP. This engine was the successor to the famous Alvis Speed Twenty. It had three SU carburettors and drove the 4·11 (or optional 4·33) rear axle through a synchromesh four-speed gearbox. The 10 ft 4 in wheelbase chassis had independent front suspension. Model shown cost £700. There were also a Drop-head Coupé and a Four-light Saloon, both costing £850.

41A: **Armstrong Siddeley** 14 HP Saloon. This was the smallest car in the company's 1937 production programme, with 9 ft wheelbase and 1666-cc (61 × 95·25 mm) six-cylinder engine. Largest was a 30 HP 12 ft wheelbase chassis with 5-litre engine.

41B: **Austin** Ten was available as Saloon, named Cambridge (shown) and Cabriolet, named Conway. The latter was similar to the saloon, except that the roof portion could be rolled back from windscreen to boot. They had a 21-bhp 1125-cc side-valve engine and four-speed gearbox. With the exception of the 7 HP models, all Austin cars had pressed steel spoke wheels ('easy clean' type). Ten models had 5·25-16 types; the similar looking but larger Twelves and Fourteens had size 5·75-16.

41C: **Austin** Ten, converted to Mobile Canteen Unit in 1939/40. The Salvation Army operated many vehicles with this type of bodywork. This particular one was presented by The Lord Mayor of Liverpool's War Fund.

41D: **Austin** Fourteen Goodwood Saloon, Series FR, was in production from August 1936 until 1939. It had a 1711-cc six-cylinder side-valve engine, four-speed gearbox, 9 ft $3\frac{3}{4}$ in wheelbase and 5·75-16 ELP (extra low pressure) tyres. In September 1937 an aluminium cylinder head was introduced.

41B Austin Ten

41C Austin Ten

41A Armstrong Siddeley 14 HP

41D Austin Fourteen

# 1937

42A: **Bentley** $4\frac{1}{4}$-Litre Allweather (convertible saloon) was offered directly by Bentley Motors, at £1645. Bodywork was 'by a well-known coachbuilder' (probably Vanden Plas) and had four doors. Engine was 4257-cc (89 × 114 mm) Six, rated at 29·4 HP, wheelbase 10 ft 6 in. Chassis cost £1150. Similar chassis was available with 3669-cc (82·5 × 114 mm) 25·3 HP engine for £1100.
42B: **Bentley** $4\frac{1}{4}$-Litre Phaeton with coachwork by Thrupp & Maberly.
42C: **British Salmson** 12 HP Model S4C was basically still the same as introduced in 1934 (*q.v.*). Unlike its derivatives, the 14 and the 20/90, the 12 HP had a conventional beam type front axle.
42D: **British Salmson** 14 HP Model S4D Drophead Coupé and Saloon, priced at £375 and £395 respectively, had independent front suspension. Engine was 1730-cc (75 × 98 mm) Four, wheelbase 9 ft 4 in. Later the cylinder bore was reduced to 72 mm (1596 cc).

42C British Salmson 12 HP

42A Bentley $4\frac{1}{4}$-Litre

42B Bentley $4\frac{1}{4}$-Litre

42D British Salmson 14 HP

43A British Salmson 20/90

43B Daimler Light Straight Eight

43C Ford Eight

43D Ford Ten

43A: **British Salmson** 20/90 had 2590-cc (75 × 98 mm) Six engine, rated at 20·8 HP, and independent front suspension. Wheelbase was 9 ft 4 in. Prices, Two-seater Sports £645, Sports Saloon (illustrated) and Coupé £695.
43B: **Daimler** Light Straight Eight chassis with James Young Sports Saloon coachwork (artist's impression).
43C: **Ford** Eight, Model 7Y, replaced the Model Y Popular during 1937 (for 1938). It was mechanically similar, having a 7 ft 6 in wheelbase chassis with transverse springing and 933-cc (56·6 × 92·5 mm) side-valve Four engine, rated at 7·96 HP. Gearbox was three-speed, tyre size 4·50-17. The new Eight had modernized body styling and pressed steel wheels. There was also a 5-cwt Van variant.
43D: **Ford** Ten, Model 7W, superseded the Model C De Luxe in May, 1937. It was distinguishable from the Model 7Y Eight by its radiator grille which had three vertical divisions. The engine was a 10 HP 1172-cc (63·5 × 92·5 mm) side-valve Four, similar to that of the preceding Model C. Wheelbase was 7 ft 10 in.

## 1937

44A: **Ford** Model 62 had 22 HP 2·2-litre V8 engine and was first introduced in 1936. Wheelbase was 9 ft 0¼ in. Specimen shown has wartime blackout markings (white-painted bumpers, etc.) and lighting.
44B: **Ford** Model 62, three-quarter rear view. The Saloon was the only body style offered and cost £210. The chassis was, however, available for special bodywork and was priced at £160. Very much the same car was produced by Matford (Mathis/Ford) in France.
44C: **Ford** 30 HP, Model 78, was available with a variety of body styles. Most were imported from Canada. It is believed that only the Sedan (saloon) was assembled at the Dagenham Ford plant. This surviving Three-window Coupé carries non-original bodywork.
44D: **Frazer-Nash** Shelsley model was a supercharged two-seater, suitable for both road work and production sports car events (Brooklands, Shelsley Walsh and other hill climbs, speed trials, road races and similar events). The 1496-cc four-cylinder engine was the same as used in the TT Replica and Ulster 100 models, except for the twin-supercharging equipment. It had a tubular front axle with inverted semi-elliptic leaf springs, acting as cantilevers, and adjustable rigid radius rods below the axle. In touring trim (£850) the car had a maximum road speed of 105 mph.

44A Ford V8 Model 62

44C Ford V8 Model 78

44B Ford V8 Model 62

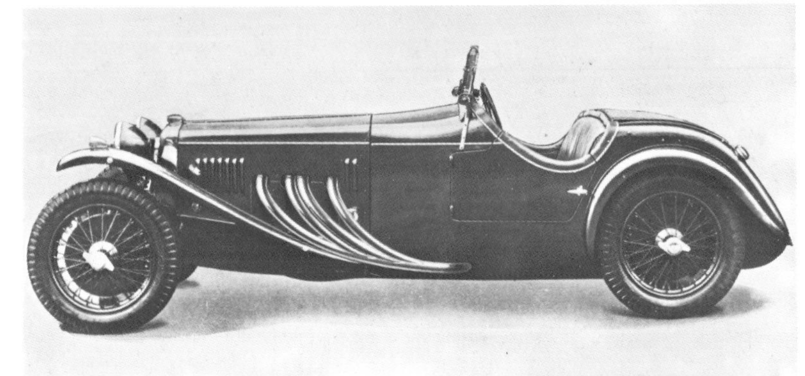
44D Frazer-Nash Shelsley

45A: **Frazer-Nash** Falcon Sports Roadster cost £425 and was particularly suitable for club competitions and trials. It had a 1911-cc (65 × 96 mm) OHV six-cylinder engine with three Solex carburettors, but was also available with the alternative OHV 1496-cc Four with twin SUs, at £450.
45B: **Hillman** Minx Magnificent was much like the 1936 model but incorporated various detail improvements. Externally it was recognisable by the five horizontal chrome-plated strips on the radiator grille. Body styles: Saloon (£163; De Luxe, as shown, £175), Drophead Coupé (£215), Tourer (£175, De Luxe £190). The Saloon could also be bought after a down-payment of £40 15s, followed by 24 monthly payments of £5 15 8d.
45C: **Hillman** Sixteen Wingham Cabriolet sold at £395 and constituted 'an open tourer and a saloon in one body, being rapidly opened or shut'. In their styling the six-cylinder Hillmans looked like scaled-up Minxes or, more accurately, Humber Eighteens with Hillman trimmings. Like the Humber they had Evenkeel independent front suspension.
45D: **Hillman** Hawk was similar to the Sixteen but had 20·92 HP 3181-cc vs. 16·95 HP 2576-cc engine. Both were side-valve Sixes. This four-door Saloon was priced at £295 (same as Sixteen Saloon).

45A Frazer-Nash Falcon

45C Hillman Sixteen

45B Hillman Minx

45D Hillman Hawk

## 1937

46A Humber Snipe

46B Humber Pullman

46C Humber Pullman

46A: **Humber** 1937 range comprised Twelve, Eighteen, Snipe and Pullman models. The former two were in their last year. Illustrated is a Foursome Drophead Coupé which was available on the Eighteen and Snipe chassis. These models differed mainly in engine size. The former had a 2731-cc unit with 69·5-mm bore and 120-mm stroke, the latter had the same stroke but 85-mm bore, resulting in a cubic capacity of 4085·7 cc.
46B: **Humber** Pullman had same engine as Snipe but 11 ft instead of 10 ft 4 in wheelbase and 7·50-16 instead of 7·00-16 tyres. Limousine shown had standard bodywork.
46C: **Humber** Pullman chassis cost £425 and was used for special bodywork. Shown is a stately Limousine by Thrupp & Maberly.
46D: **Jensen** 3½-Litre was luxurious Anglo-American high-performance car. It had a 30 HP Ford V-8-cylinder engine of 3621-cc cubic capacity with three-speed remote-control gearbox and Columbia two-speed rear axle (4·11 and 2·9 to 1). Road speed with 'pre-selective overdrive top' (2·9 to 1) was 60 mph at 2000 rpm. Saloon shown cost £695. Sports Tourer (£645) and Drophead Coupé (£765) were also available.

46D Jensen 3½-Litre

47A: **Jowett** 7G was powered by the rugged little 946-cc flat-twin, rated at 7·35 HP. Car was larger and roomier than other 'Eights'. A Four (7J) was available, too. Both had 8 ft 6 in wheelbase.
47B: **Lanchester** Eleven Sportsman's Coupé, a one-off model which has survived in Devon, serving one family from new. The 10·8 HP four-cylinder engine has overhead valves and is of 1444-cc (66 × 105 mm) cubic capacity. Transmission is of the Daimler Fluid Flywheel type with four forward speeds. The chassis was priced at £215 and factory-supplied bodies included Saloons and Coupés from £298 up to £325.
47C: **Lanchester** Eighteen with Six-Light Saloon coachwork. This model had a 2565-cc (72 × 105 mm) six-cylinder engine, four-speed Fluid Flywheel transmission and 9 ft 6 in wheelbase. The chassis price was £435.
47D: **MG** T-Series Model TA Midget Two-seater. The TA was in production during 1936-39 and was developed from the preceding Model PB. Price in October 1937 was £222.

47A Jowett 7G

47C Lanchester Eighteen

47B Lanchester Eleven

47D MG Midget

# 1937

48A: **MG** VA-Series 1½-Litre range comprised Saloon, Tourer (shown) and Convertible models. They were in production during 1937-39 and were similar to the 1936-39 SA-Series (*q.v.*) but with 9 ft wheelbase and 1548-cc 55-bhp four-cylinder engine. The chassis cost £215, the Tourer £280.
48B: **MG** SA-Series 2-Litre Saloon had six-cylinder engine of 2288-cc capacity and was priced at £389. The 10 ft 3 in wheelbase chassis cost £260.
48C: **Morgan** introduced their first four-wheeler in 1936 but the three-wheelers for which the Company had become famous were continued. The 1937 Model 4/4 (four cylinders, four speeds, four wheels) was an improved version of the 1936 model. It had a 34-bhp 1122-cc (63 × 90 mm) Coventry Climax engine with overhead inlet, side exhaust valves. Wheelbase was 7 ft 8 in, tyre size 5·50-16.
48D: **Morris** Eight Series II Saloon featured 'easy-clean' wheels and a painted radiator shell, otherwise was much like the preceding Series I. This beautifully preserved two-door Saloon registered in December 1937, was photographed in 1972. It was strictly a 1938 model.

48A MG 1½-Litre

48B MG 2-Litre

48C Morgan 4/4

48D Morris Eight

49A Morris Series II

49B Riley Sprite

49C Riley 15 HP

49D Rolls-Royce Phantom III

49A: **Morris** continued their Series II models (and Eight Series I) with only minor changes until about mid-year when a new range of bigger Morrises, designated Series III, appeared. They differed from the Series II (shown) in having OHV engines, 'easy-clean' wheels, etc. (*see* 1938). Car shown is carried on a special winch-equipped transporter, towed by a Scammell 'Mechanical Horse' three-wheeled tractive unit.
49B: **Riley** Sprite Open Two-seater had twin-carburettor $1\frac{1}{2}$-litre (1496-cc, 69 × 100 mm) 12 HP OHV four-cylinder engine and pre-selector gearbox. It was in production during 1936-38.
49C: **Riley** 15 HP model had a 1726-cc six-cylinder engine and in saloon form cost £380. The company also produced a few models with 18 HP V-8-cylinder engines. These engines were made up of two 9 HP blocks and had a cubic capacity of 2178 cc (60·3 × 95·2 mm).
49D: **Rolls-Royce** 40/50 HP Phantom III Sedanca Coupé. This superb motor car had a 7340-cc (82·5 × 114 mm) 12-cylinder engine, rated at 50·7 HP. The chassis alone cost £1900. Wheelbase was 11 ft 10 in, tyre size 7·00-18. Two other Rolls-Royce chassis which were available were the 20/25 HP (3669-cc Six, £1050) and the 25/30 HP (4257-cc Six, £1100), both with 11 ft wheelbase and 6·00-19 tyres.

## 1937

50A: **Rolls-Royce** 40/50 HP Phantom III Limousine. Coachwork shown in this artist's impression was by Thrupp & Maberly.
50B: **Rover** 1937/38 range had various styling changes. There were Ten, Twelve, Fourteen, Sixteen and Speed models. Illustrated is a Twelve Sports Saloon with 1938-style plain-sided bonnet. It had a four-cylinder engine of 1496-cc capacity (69 × 100 mm), rated at 11·9 HP. Gearbox was four-speed, wheelbase 9 ft 4 in, tyres 5·00-18.

50C: **Singer** Nine had 972-cc (60 × 86 mm) four-cylinder engine and 7 ft 7 in wheelbase. During 1937 the pressed steel wheels (shown) replaced the earlier wire spoke type. Basic models were known as Bantam.
50D: **Singer** Twelve Saloon had $1\frac{1}{2}$-litre four-cylinder OHV engine, four-speed gearbox, 8 ft 7 in wheelbase and 5·25-16 tyres on pressed steel wheels. It cost £225. Picture was taken at Darricot Hill.

50A Rolls-Royce Phantom III

50C Singer Nine

50B Rover Twelve

50D Singer Twelve

51A: **Singer** Nine Four-seater Sports Model cost £195 and had 972-cc engine, rated at 8·93 HP. Wheelbase was 7 ft 7 in.
51B: **Singer** $1\frac{1}{2}$-Litre four-cylinder 2/4-seater sports car, one of the only six (two teams of three) built.
51C: **SS** Jaguar 100 sold at £395 and had basically the same 19·8 HP engine (2663·7-cc, 73×106 mm) as the firm's $2\frac{1}{2}$-Litre Saloon. Wheelbase was 8 ft 6 in, tyre size 5·25-18. Plaques on the wall indicate the registered offices of Swallow Coachbuilding Company Ltd and SS Cars Ltd.
51D: **SS** Jaguar $2\frac{1}{2}$-Litre was a very elegant sports saloon. It was first introduced in 1936 and was the first SS for which the name Jaguar was used. Its 2663·7-cc engine was made by Standard. A $1\frac{1}{2}$-Litre variant was also available.

51A Singer Nine

51B Singer $1\frac{1}{2}$-Litre

51C SS Jaguar 100

51D SS Jaguar $2\frac{1}{2}$-Litre

52A Standard Flying V8

52C Talbot Ten

52B Talbot Ten

52A: **Standard** Flying V8 Saloon was unveiled at 1936 Olympia Motor Show with a price tag of £349. It was in limited production for only two years. Shown is a 1938-registered specimen which was still operational thirty years later. The 20 HP 2686-cc (63·5 × 106 mm) side-valve power unit did not look unlike a Ford V8 but was in fact based on two 10 HP cylinder blocks. It was claimed it could attain 82 mph. A Drophead Coupé variant was offered at £359. Wheelbase was 8 ft 6 in.
52B: **Talbot** Ten Sports Tourer (shown) and Sports Saloon both sold for £248. The third model in the range, a Drophead Foursome Coupé was priced at £278. They had a 9·8 HP 1185-cc side-valve engine with four-speed gearbox and different final drive ratios for open and closed cars. Wheelbase was 7 ft 9 in, tyre size 5·25-16.
52C: **Talbot** Ten Sports Tourers serving as police patrol cars in Norfolk. Note wheel discs.
52D: **Talbot** 75 Six-light Saloon cost £485 in 1936, £425 in 1937. It had a 17·9 HP six-cylinder engine. Most expensive Talbot was 24 HP Limousine, at £795 (1936: £895). Picture was taken at Penshurst, Kent.

52D Talbot 75

53A Triumph Dolomite

53B Vauxhall 25 HP

53C Vauxhall 25 HP

53B-C: **Vauxhall** 25 HP G-Series was continued in short- (shown) and long-wheelbase variants. Other 1937 Vauxhalls were the D-Series 12 and 14 HP. During 1937 the company introduced a new 10 HP, the H-Series, which featured integral body-cum-chassis construction (*see* 1938).

53D: **Wolseley** 12/48 Series II sold at £225 in Saloon form and had a 12 HP 1547-cc (69·5 × 102 mm) four-cylinder OHV engine, four-speed gearbox, 8 ft 4 in wheelbase and 5·75-16 tyres on pressed-steel wheels. The chassis was available at £160 and a Coupé at £257 10s. Other Wolseleys in the 1937 programme were the 10/40, 14/56, Sixteen, 21 and 25 HP.

53A: **Triumph** offerings for 1937 included Gloria, Vitesse, Dolomite and Continental models, priced from £268 upwards. The Gloria had a 1232-cc Coventry Climax Four engine, the Continental a 1991-cc Triumph OHV Six. The intermediate models could be had with either a 1767-cc Four or the 1991-cc Six Triumph engine.

53D Wolseley 12/48

**1938** Although the number of vehicles on the roads of the United Kingdom was now over 2½ million (1,984,430 cars, 89,410 'hackneys', 504,028 commercials), both production and exports showed a downward trend.
1938 production of cars dropped to 341,028, that of trucks and buses to 103,849. Exports of cars dropped from 78,113 to 68,257 units. In order to make British cars more attractive in export markets, several manufacturers had for some time been producing engines with a large cylinder bore (which, within the United Kingdom, resulted in higher road tax, the taxation system being based mainly on the cylinder bore). Conversely, several American cars had been or were available with special 'tax-cheating' small-bore engines. New vehicle registrations during 1938 totalled 427,578 and included 280,217 cars and 8,843 'hackneys'.

54B AC 16/60

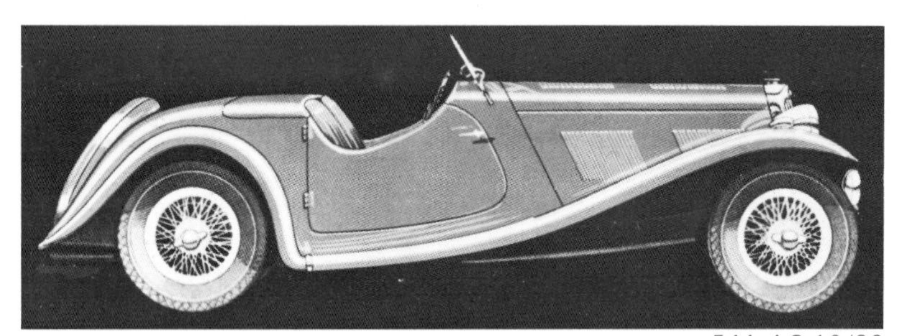

54A AC 16/80

54C Alvis Silver Crest

54A: **AC** (Acedes) Cars Ltd offered 16/60, 16/70 and 16/80 chassis and a variety of body styles. Illustrated is the Two-Seater Sports Competition model on the 16/80 chassis. It was capable of a cruising speed of 90 mph, 'under favourable conditions'. A 16/70 Four-Seater version was available also. Both were priced at £500.
54B: **AC** 16/60 Five-Passenger Wide Track Greyhound Saloon was company's topline model, costing £585. It had 9 ft 11 in wheelbase and 4 ft 5 in track, compared with 9 ft 7 in and 4 ft 2 in on other models (except Two-Seater Competition Sports which had 8 ft 10 in wheelbase).
54C: **Alvis** Silver Crest was a six-cylinder engine chassis and George Lanchester had a great deal of say in the design of it. The Alvis 12/70 shared the same basic engineering but had only four cylinders. The Silver Crest Drophead Coupé shown had bodywork by Tickford.
54D: **Armstrong Siddeley** 17 HP chassis had 2394-cc (66·67 × 114 mm) six-cylinder engine and four-speed gearbox. Car illustrated had Landaulette coachwork by Salmons & Sons of Newport Pagnell, Bucks.

54D Armstrong Siddeley 17 HP

55A Austin Seven

55B Austin Fourteen

55C Austin Eighteen

55A: **Austin** Seven was in its last full year. There were Saloon (Model ARR, shown), Cabriolet (AC), Tourer (AAL) and Two-seater (APE) body styles. From July they had full Girling brakes and concealed bonnet hinges. In 1939 the Seven and the 7·99 HP Big Seven were superseded by a new Eight.

55B: **Austin** Fourteen Goodwood Cabriolet was similar to Fourteen Goodwood Saloon except for the roll-back roof as shown. Wheelbase was 9 ft 4 in. Engine was a 1711-cc (65·5 × 84·63 mm) side valve Six, developing 52 bhp and rated at 15·96 HP. Ten Cambridge Saloon and Conway Cabriolet looked similar but were somewhat smaller and had four-cylinder 32-bhp power unit.

55C: **Austin** Eighteen Iver was a seven-seater Limousine on 10 ft 3 in wheelbase chassis, powered by a 65-bhp 17·9 HP side-valve six engine of 2510-cc capacity (69·35 × 111 mm). Without sliding glass partition it was known as the Windsor Saloon, with 9 ft 4½ in wheelbase (five-seater) as the Norfolk. Car shown is owned by Mr Sly of Minehead in Somerset and has covered well over 500,000 miles.

55D: **British Salmson** range comprised S4C 12 HP, S4D 14 HP and 20/90 models, all shown in this period advertisement. The former two had four-cylinder engines, rated at 11·9 and 12·8 HP respectively. The 20/90 was a Six and was the only model continued for 1939.

55E: **British Salmson** 20/90 Six-Cylinder Two-Seater Sports. This attractive model sold at £645. The 20/90 was mechanically similar to the 14 HP with the main exception of the engine. Both had 9 ft 4¼ in wheelbase.

55D British Salmson 12 HP, 14 HP and 20/90

55E British Salmson 20/90

56A BSA Scout

56B BSA Scout

56C Daimler Six

56A: **BSA** Scout Series 4 Two-Seater De Luxe cost £156 10s and had an aluminium-panelled body with frame of selected ash. It had a three-speed gearbox with dash-mounted remote control, and front-wheel drive. Engine was 1203-cc (63·5 x 95 mm) side-valve Four. Four-seater version available also, both in standard and de luxe form. All Scouts had independent front suspension with quarter-elliptic leaf springs.

56B: **BSA** Scout Coupé De Luxe sold at £179 but could be ordered with twin carburettors for £5 5s extra. It was a two-seater with large luggage space behind the bench-type seat and had a sliding roof as standard equipment.

56C: **Daimler** Roadster with Charlesworth bodywork with Mr R. S. (Bob) Crouch (later Daimler bus sales manager) who rallied it during 1938/39. In 1938 Daimler offered three Sixes (16·2, 19·3 and 23·8 HP) and two in-line Eights (25·7 and 31·7 HP). Car shown is strictly a 1939 model.

56D: **Daimler** Light Straight Eight chassis had 10 ft 3 in wheelbase and was used by several well-known coachbuilders, including Arthur Mulliner, Vanden Plas, James Young, Freestone & Webb, Salmons & Sons, etc. The engine was an OHV straight-eight of 3421-cc capacity (72 x 105 mm), rated at 25·7 HP. Like all contemporary Daimlers it had Fluid Flywheel transmission incorporating four-speed pre-selective epicyclic gearbox. Rear axle was underslung three-quarter floating worm driven type.

56D Daimler Light Straight Eight

57A Daimler Light Straight Eight

57B Ford Ten

57D Ford V8 Model 81A

57A: **Daimler** Light Straight Eight with Pillarless Saloon coachwork by Vanden Plas (England) 1923 Ltd.
57B: **Ford** Ten, Model 7W, was available as Saloon and Four-seater Tourer (shown). It had the familiar 1172-cc side-valve Four engine.
57C: **Ford** 22 HP V8 Model 62 was basically similar to 1936/37 model but had larger boot and detail modifications. Bumper overriders were no longer fitted and the small circular grilles below the headlights incorporated V8 emblems. Prices were up by £30 and the Saloon now cost £240.
57D: **Ford** 30 HP V8 Model 81A, delivered to the British Army. Basically the North American Ford V8 Station Wagon this particular RHD model was fitted with 9·00-13 (vs. 6·00-16) tyres and the wing cut-outs were enlarged to provide extra clearance. Other British fittings were the semaphore type direction indicators and the wing-mounted sidelights.

57C Ford V8 Model 62

57E: **Frazer-Nash** Colmore had a three/four-seater touring body. It cost £550 and is shown here with full weather protection installed. The wheelbase was 9 ft, the standard engine a 1657-cc (60 × 97·9 mm) twin-OHC Blackburne Six with two SU carburettors. Four-cylinder power units were also available. Like all Frazer-Nashes it had an unorthodox transmission system with dog-clutch gear-change and separate chains for each of the four forward ratios to the differential-less rear axle.

57E Frazer-Nash Colmore

## 1938

58A Hillman 'Little Jim'

58B Hillman 'Little Jim'

58D Hillman Minx

58C Hillman Minx

58A-B: **Hillman** 'Little Jim', earliest ancestor of the Imp? Only two prototypes were produced in about 1938 but for some reason or other the project was cancelled and the cars were subsequently dismantled. Shown is the unitary construction bodyshell of what would seem to have been an attractive looking little car.
58C: **Hillman** Minx 1938 models had a restyled radiator grille and full-width bumpers. Illustrated is the Drophead Coupé, the top of which could be adjusted to three individual positions, open, de Ville (shown) and closed. It was priced at £215.
58D: **Hillman** Minx Saloon in the 1938 Monte Carlo Rally. It was driven by the well-known Dutch driver Maus Gatsonides who covered the route without loss of marks. The car is seen here at the Bulgaria-Yugoslavia frontier, together with another Dutch entry (1937 Ford V8 Coupé).

59A: **Hillman** Fourteen Saloon had 13·9 HP four-cylinder engine, all-synchromesh gearbox, Evenkeel independent front suspension and other refinements. Tyres were 5·75-16 on pressed steel wheels. Radiator grille was similar to that of the Minx. Prices £248 to £268.
59B: **Hillman** Seven-Seater was company's last Six. Saloon cost £375, Limousine version £395. Wheelbase was 10 ft 6 in, engine 3181-cc (75 × 120 mm) side-valve six-cylinder, same as Humber Snipe.
59C: **Humber** Sixteen Saloon was lowest-priced six-cylinder Humber so far, at £330. Except for engine, radiator grille and minor details it resembled the Hillman Fourteen (*q.v.*). The radiator grille was similar to that of the Snipe. Engine was a 2576·5-cc (67·5 × 120 mm) side-valve unit, rated at 16·95 HP. Wheelbase was 9 ft 6 in, tyre size 6·00-16.
59D: **Humber** Snipe chassis was now offered in two versions, viz. the 20·9 HP shown here and the larger Snipe Imperial (*q.v.*). The 20·9 HP resembled the Humber Sixteen but had 75-mm cylinder bore, resulting in 3181-cc cubic capacity. Wheelbase was 9 ft 6 in and the Saloon shown cost £345.
59E: **Humber** Snipe Imperial Six-light Saloon with sliding roof cost £495. The 4085·7-cc engine (85 × 120 mm) was rated at 26·88 HP and was the same as used in the Pullman chassis. Tyre size was 7·00-16, wheelbase 10 ft 4 in.

59A Hillman Fourteen

59C Humber Sixteen

59D Humber Snipe

59B Hillman Seven-Seater

59E Humber Snipe Imperial

60A: **Humber** Snipe Imperial with attractive Sports Saloon bodywork, priced at £565. It is shown at the foot of Bwlch-y-Groes, a well-known mountain pass in North Wales.
60B: **Humber** Snipe Imperial Drophead Coupé with three-position convertible top. This model sold at £555.
60C-D: **Humber** Pullman chassis had 11 ft wheelbase and 7·50-16 tyres but otherwise its technical specification was much like that of the Snipe Imperial. Shown are two typical examples of Thrupp & Maberly coachwork on this chassis.

60A Humber Snipe Imperial

60B Humber Snipe Imperial

60C Humber Pullman

60D Humber Pullman

61A: **Lagonda** offered six- and V-12-cylinder chassis. Shown is a Drophead Coupé on the former, which carried model designation LG6. The chassis prices were £875 and £895 for 10 ft $7\frac{1}{2}$ in and 11 ft $3\frac{1}{2}$ in wheelbase size respectively. Engine was a 4453-cc (88·5 × 120·64 mm) OHV unit, rated at 29·13 HP. Complete cars cost from £1150 up to £1540. V-12 chassis (4480 cc) were priced from £1200 up to £1250, depending on wheelbase, complete cars from £1485 to £1875.
61B: **MG** VA-Series $1\frac{1}{2}$-Litre had four-cylinder 1548-cc (69·5 × 102 mm) OHV engine with twin SU carburettors, developing 55 bhp at 4400 rpm. Saloon, Tourer (shown) and Drophead Coupé body styles were offered and some 2400 were produced during 1937-39.
61C: **MG** VA-Series $1\frac{1}{2}$-Litre Drophead Coupé. The SA-Series 2-Litre models (1936-39) were similar in appearance but had longer wheelbase and six-cylinder engines.
61D: **Morgan** 4/4 had 9·8 HP Coventry Climax four-cylinder engine, four-speed gearbox and spiral bevel final drive. Shown is the Drophead Coupé body style which was in production for many years.

61A Lagonda LG6

61C MG $1\frac{1}{2}$-Litre

61B MG $1\frac{1}{2}$-Litre

61D Morgan 4/4

## 1938

62A: **Morris** display of 1938 models. On the right is a Series II Eight Saloon. Next to it are three Series III Ten-Fours and, at the end, a Fourteen-Six. For 1938 all Morrises had painted radiator shells.
62B: **Morris** Ten-Four, Series III, had same bodywork as Series II of 1936/37, but featured various detail modifications. The engine was a four-cylinder 1292-cc (63·5 × 120 mm) unit, rated at 10·0 HP. Wheelbase was 8 ft 4 in, tyre size 5·50-16.
62C: **Morris** Fourteen Six, Series III, export model differed from home market cars in various details. This early specimen, fitted with Ace wheel discs, has survived and was photographed in 1972.
62D: **Morris** Twenty-Five, Series III, looked like a stretched Fourteen Six and had built-out luggage boot. Wheelbase was 10 ft 1½ in, tyre size 7·00-16. Engine was a 3485-cc (82 × 110 mm) OHV Six, rated at 25·01 HP. Saloon cost £320.
62E: **Morris** Twenty-Five, Series III, Special Coupé. It sold at £345. Optional extra equipment included a folding luggage grid at rear. Mechanically it was similar to the Twenty-Five Saloon.

62B Morris Ten-Four

62C Morris Fourteen Six

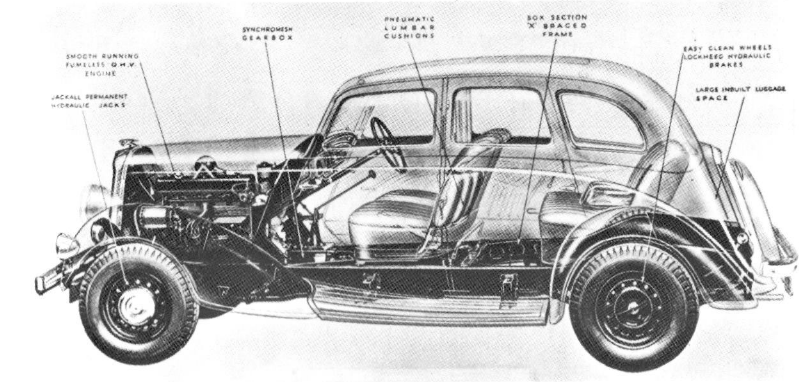

62D Morris Twenty-Five

62A Morris Series II and III

62E Morris Twenty-Five

63A Railton 28·8 HP

63B Rolls-Royce 25/30 HP

63C Rolls-Royce Phantom III

63D Rolls-Royce Phantom III

63A: **Railton** was Anglo-American ('hybrid') car produced in Cobham, Surrey. Chassis and engine were Hudson Terraplane (4168-cc side-valve straight-eight). This somewhat modified early specimen of the marque was photographed at a rally in 1970. The chassis price in 1938 was £438 for 10 ft 2 in wheelbase, £540 for 10 ft 9 in.
63B: **Rolls-Royce** 25/30 HP 11 ft wheelbase chassis with Park Ward All-Weather coachwork. The 25/30 HP had a 4257-cc (89 × 114 mm) six-cylinder engine and 6·00-19 tyres. The bare chassis cost £1100.
63C: **Rolls-Royce** 40/50 HP Phantom III had a V-12-cylinder engine of 7340-cc cubic capacity (82·5 × 114 mm), rated at 50·7 HP. As usual, Rolls-Royce did not disclose the actual power output; it was considered 'quite adequate'.
63D: **Rolls-Royce** 40/50 HP Phantom III had 10 in longer wheelbase and six more cylinders than the 25/30 HP. The tyre size was 7·00-18 and the bare chassis cost £1900. A factory-supplied Saloon cost £2675, a Limousine £2670.

# 1938

64A: **Rolls-Royce** Phantom III with Sedanca de Ville Coachwork in the Netherlands.
64B: **Rover** Ten Saloon had four-cylinder OHV engine, rated at 10·9 HP. Cubic capacity was 1389·28 cc (66·5 × 100 mm). Wheelbase was 8 ft 9 in, tyre size 4·75-18. Price £255.
64C: **Rover** Twelve Sports Saloon was a four-light model but was also available as a six-light Saloon. Prices were £310 and £300 respectively. Power unit was a 1495·72-cc (69 × 100 mm) OHV Four. Wheelbase 9 ft 4 in. Tyres 5·25-17. Fourteen and Sixteen models looked much the same and were also available as Six-light or Four-light Sports Saloons. The top-line Twenty, or Speed, was a larger-bore version of the Sixteen, available only as Sports Saloon (£425).
64D: **Singer** Bantam De Luxe had a new 8·93 HP 1074-cc four-cylinder OHC engine. It cost £149 10s. Available for £10 less was the Bantam Popular which was similar but did not have the De Luxe's sliding roof, luggage carrier, leather seating and bumpers. Both had three-speed gearbox, 7 ft 7 in wheelbase and 5·00-16 tyres on 'easy clean' wheels.

---

64A Rolls-Royce Phantom III

64B Rover Ten

64C Rover Twelve

64D Singer Bantam

65A Singer Twelve

65A: **Singer** Twelve Drophead Coupé sold at £279 and was the company's top-line model. Mechanically it was similar to the Twelve and Super Twelve Saloons, featuring an 11·4 HP 1525-cc four-cylinder OHC engine, four-speed gearbox, semi-elliptic leaf springs front and rear and 8 ft 7 in wheelbase. Tyre size was 5·25-16 (5·50-16 on Super Twelve).

65B: **SS** Jaguar for 1938 was available in $3\frac{1}{2}$-, $2\frac{1}{2}$ and $1\frac{1}{2}$-Litre form with HP ratings of 25, 20 and 14 respectively. All engines were produced by the Standard Motor Co and incorporated Weslake patents. 'The Motor' described the Jaguar as '. . . a credit to the British Automobile Industry.'

65C: **Standard** Flying Ten Super Saloon with 1267-cc (63·5 × 100 mm) engine and four-speed gearbox. 1938 models had restyled radiator grilles. They were generally referred to as Flying Standards. The range included Flying Nine, Ten, Twelve, Fourteen and Twenty models. The latter had a six-cylinder engine, all the others were Fours. The limited-production V8 (*see* 1937) was still available, at £325.

65D: **Standard** Flying Twelve was powered by a 1609-cc (69·5 × 106 mm) four-cylinder side-valve engine and cost £205. A Drophead Coupé variant was also available.

65B SS Jaguar

65C Standard Flying Ten

65D Standard Flying Twelve

66A: **Standard** Flying Fourteen was company's largest four-cylinder model (1776-cc, 73 x 106 mm). Wheelbase was 9 ft. As can be seen, all models bore a strong family resemblance.
66B: **Talbot** 1938 models at the Earls Court Motor Show in October 1937. In the centre is the then-new 3-Litre Saloon which was based on the Humber Super Snipe. On the right is the Ten Sports Tourer, based on the Hillman Minx. (Like Hillman and Humber, the Clement Talbot company was part of the Rootes Group; later in the year the company and the cars were re-named Sunbeam-Talbot).
66C: **Talbot** 3-Litre Sports Tourers at the entrance of the impressive Clement Talbot Motor Works (later the Rootes service department) in Barlby Road, Ladbroke Grove, London W10.
66D: **Triumph** offered Dolomite, Vitesse and Gloria models. Various types of engines were available. Shown is the Dolomite 2-Litre Saloon which had a 15·72 HP 1991-cc (65 x 100 mm) six-cylinder OHV engine. It was optionally available with a four-cylinder engine of 1767-cc (75 x 100 mm, 13·95 HP) or 1496-cc (69 x 100 mm, 11·81 HP) capacity. All power units were now of Triumph design and manufacture. Wheelbase was 9 ft 8 in, tyre size 5·50-17.

66A Standard Flying Fourteen

66B Talbot Ten and 3-Litre

66C Talbot 3-Litre

66D Triumph Dolomite

67A Triumph Vitesse

67A: **Triumph** Vitesse 14/60 4-Window Saloon had the 1767-cc Four engine, 9 ft wheelbase and 5·00-17 tyres. In 2-Litre six-cylinder form it looked generally similar but the wheelbase (and bonnet) were 8 in longer and the tyre size was 5·25-17.

67B: **Vauxhall** Ten, H-Series, Model HI Saloon, also known as Ten-Four. This was the first British car with unitary body-cum-chassis construction and it remained in production until the war, after which it was continued until 1947 as Model HIY. Produced concurrently with the H-Series 10 HP was the I-Series 12 HP. Both had Dubonnet-type independent front suspension with torsion bars.

67C: **Vauxhall** 25 HP, G-Series, Model GY Saloon. It had a wheelbase length of 9 ft 3 in but was available also with 10 ft 10 in wheelbase, designated Model GL. Both had a 3215-cc OHV Six engine and independent front suspension. Prices, GY Saloon £315, GL Grosvenor Limousine £595. Special coachwork on this chassis included a Tickford Foursome Coupé by Salmons & Sons (£410), four-door Wingham Cabriolet by Martin Walter (£415) and Grosvenor Close-Coupled Sports Saloon (£385).

67B Vauxhall Ten

67D Wolseley Twenty-Five

67E Wolseley Twenty-Five

67C Vauxhall 25 HP

67D: **Wolseley** Twenty-Five Super Six, Series III, had 3485-cc (82 × 110 mm) OHV six-cylinder engine, rated at 25·01 HP, four-speed gearbox, 9 ft $9\frac{1}{2}$ in wheelbase (Limousine variant 12 ft $1\frac{1}{4}$ in). All models had illuminated Wolseley badge on radiator grille.

67E: **Wolseley** Super Sixes all looked alike. Differences were mainly in engine cubic capacity (1818 to 3485 cc). Wheelbase of Saloon models was 8 ft 10 in for 14/56 and 18/80 models, 9 ft $9\frac{1}{2}$ in for 16, 21 and 25 HP. Shown is a 25 HP with 7·00-16 tyres.

**1939** This was the year the second World War started. For the United Kingdom and the Commonwealth it began in September and the motor industry became a major contributor of war materials. These did not only comprise trucks and other transport but tanks and armoured cars, aircraft and aircraft engines, guns and ammunition, and countless other items. Armoured fighting vehicle production immediately got underway and during September to December 947 AFVs were built, followed by 7441 in 1940 and then rising steadily to 31,851 in 1943. Export of cars and trucks still amounted to 77,412 units, valued at £9.7 million; obviously for 1940 these figures were considerably lower. By the end of November 2,157,975 vehicles were in use in the United Kingdom, namely 1,627,083 private cars, 463,474 commercials and only 67,418 'hackneys' (lowest since 1919). Large numbers of private cars and trucks were impressed by the armed forces and many civilian cars were transformed into ambulances, American cars being particularly suitable for such conversions. Approximately 305,000 cars were produced during this year and new car registrations amounted to 235,795 plus 7093 'hackneys'.

68A AC 16/80

68B Alvis 4·3-Litre

68C Alvis 4·3-Litre

68A: **AC** 16/80 Sports chassis with Four-seater Tourer bodywork. This chassis cost £350 in standard 15·7 HP form but was available with 16·9 HP Arnott supercharged engine at an extra £56. Wheelbase was 8 ft 10 in, tyre size 5·00-19. An early model is shown.
68B: **Alvis** 4·3-Litre with special Drophead Coupé coachwork. The 4·3 was available with 10 ft 4 in and 10 ft 7 in wheelbase. The engine was a 4387-cc (92 × 110 mm) OHV Six with three carbs, rated at 31·48 HP. Actual power output was 137 bhp at 3600 rpm. Front suspension was independent with transverse leaf spring, brakes were servo-assisted mechanical. Maximum speed was over 100 mph.
68C: **Alvis** 4·3-Litre Standard Four-Door Saloon cost £995. It was built on the long (10 ft 7 in wb) chassis, which cost £750 'bare'. One of these saloons lapped Brooklands at just over 103 mph.

69A Armstrong Siddeley 16 HP

69B Austin Norfolk 18 HP

69C Austin Ascot 12 HP

69A: **Armstrong Siddeley** 16 HP Saloon was new model, equipped with Wilson four-speed pre-selective gearbox with control on steering column. The engine was a 1991-cc (65×100 mm) OHV Six. Wheelbase 9 ft 3 in. Tyre size 5·50-17. Prices, chassis £275, Saloon £380. 14, 17, 20 and 25 HP models were unchanged carryovers from 1938.
69B: **Austin** 1939 range comprised more than 25 models in seven series. During the year two new models were added: a new Eight and a redesigned Ten. The other models were much the same as for 1938 but with detail improvements. Illustrated is a five-seater Norfolk Saloon on the 18 HP short wheelbase (9 ft 4½ in) chassis with 2510-cc side-valve Six engine. Permanent hydraulic jacks facilitated the raising of all four wheels or the front and rear wheels in pairs.
69C: **Austin** Ascot Cabriolet on 12 HP chassis. The folding roof could be fixed in one of three positions: up, halfway open or fully lowered. Similar-looking but of different dimensions were the Conway (10 HP) and Goodwood (14 HP) Cabriolets.
69D: **Austin** Twenty-Eight Ranelagh Limousine was company's most luxurious model and cost £700 (cheapest 1938/39 Austin was Seven Two-seater at £108). The 27·75 HP six-cylinder engine had an aluminium cylinder head and developed 90 bhp. Cubic capacity was 4016 cc, wheelbase 11 ft 4 in, tyre size 6·50-17. Glass partition, folding occasional seats and electric telephone were included in the standard specification.

69D Austin Ranelagh 28 HP

# 1939

70A: **Bentley** $4\frac{1}{4}$-Litre Sports Tourer, a full four-seater shown here with windscreen folded and tonneau cover fitted. This was one of various bodystyles available and cost £1485. The chassis was priced at £1150 and had a wheelbase of 10 ft 6 in.
70B: **Bentley** $4\frac{1}{4}$-Litre engine had 88·9 mm bore × 114·3 mm stroke, giving a swept volume of 4257 cc. Treasury rating was 29·4 HP, actual bhp figure was not disclosed. The $4\frac{1}{4}$-Litre engine was first offered in 1937, alongside the $3\frac{1}{2}$-Litre. From 1938 only the $4\frac{1}{4}$-Litre was available.
70C: **Daimler** ES24 or Twenty Four was one of the Daimler company's three six-cylinder models. The others were the Fifteen $2\frac{1}{2}$-Litre and Twenty. Engine cubic capacities were 3317, 2522 and 2565 cc respectively. There were also two eight-cylinder models, namely the 4-Litre Straight Eight (3960 cc) and the Straight Eight (4624 cc).
70D-E: **Daimler** Twenty Four Limousine as used by the Royal Air Force as AOC (Air Officer Commanding) car. The six-cylinder OHV engine developed 75 bhp at 3600 rpm and was rated at 23·81 HP. Like all other Daimler models it featured Fluid Flywheel with pre-selective epicyclic four-speed gearbox and worm-drive rear axle. Suspension was by semi-elliptic leaf springs, front and rear. Brakes were Girling mechanical with Clayton Dewandre vacuum servo assistance. Wheelbase 10 ft 4 in. Tyre size 6·50-17.

70A Bentley $4\frac{1}{4}$-Litre

70C Daimler Twenty Four

70B Bentley $4\frac{1}{4}$-Litre

70D Daimler Twenty Four

70E Daimler Twenty Four

71A Ford Eight, Prefect and V8

71B Ford Prefect

71C Ford V8 Model 91A

71A: **Ford** Motor Company Ltd of Dagenham offered four series of cars, namely the Eight, Model 7Y (later in the year superseded by the Anglia, Model E04A), the restyled 10 HP Prefect, Model E93A, the 22 HP V8, Model 62 (continued from 1938, *q.v.*) and the American type 30 HP V8, Model 91A. This advertisement of July, 1939, shows the 7Y, E93A and 91A models.

71B: **Ford** Prefect 10 HP, Model E93A, had a redesigned front end and some detail modifications, otherwise was much like the preceding Ten Model 7W (1937-38). Engine was the well-known 1172-cc (63·5 × 92·5 mm) side-valve Four, with three-speed gearbox. Wheelbase was 7 ft 10 in, tyre size 4·50-17.

71C: **Ford** V8 30 HP, Model 91A, Four-door Saloon was similar to its North American counterpart, the 91A-73 Fordor Sedan. In fact, it was an RHD assembled product using components imported from Canada. It was the first Ford car to have hydraulic brakes.

72A Hillman Minx

72A: **Hillman** Minx for 1939 featured some detail changes, including a restyled dashboard. The 1184·5-cc side-valve Four engine was retained, but a redesigned gearbox with synchromesh on second, third and top gear was introduced. The basic Saloon cost £163.
72B: **Hillman** Minx Saloon of Mr W. M. Couper (right) who won his class with it in the 1939 Monte Carlo Rally.
72C: **Hillman** Fourteen Four was the only other Hillman model produced besides the Minx; the Sixes had disappeared in favour of the Humber Sixteen and Snipe. Car shown was in service with the Admiralty (Royal Navy). During the early days of World War II it was fitted, as shown, with roof protection against shrapnel. Note also the white paint markings all around the car. This was obligatory during the blackout period.

72B Hillman Minx

72D Humber Snipe

72E Humber Super Snipe

72C Hillman Fourteen

72D: **Humber** Sixteen, Snipe and Super Snipe for 1939 were all similar in appearance. All had 9 ft 6 in wheelbase and 6·00-16 tyres. Main difference was under the bonnet where the six-cylinder side-valve engines were of 2576·5-, 3180·9- and 4085·7-cc cubic capacity. All had 120-mm stroke, bore being 67·5, 75 and 85 mm respectively.
72E: **Humber** started military (Super) Snipe Mk 2 production in the Summer of 1939. Shown is a Utility vehicle as supplied to the War Office. It had large (9·00-13) tyres, wire mesh type radiator grille and other military modifications. Other body styles on the same chassis: Staff Saloon, Open Tourer, 8-cwt Truck, Light Reconnaissance Car, etc. In War Office nomenclature the word 'Super' was usually omitted from the vehicle model designation although all had the 85-mm bore engine.

73A: **Humber** Pullman had same 4085·7-cc six-cylinder engine as Super Snipe and Imperial but 11 ft wheelbase. Shown is a Limousine by Thrupp & Maberly.
73B: **Lagonda** Saloon de Ville was available with V-12-cylinder engine and 11 ft wheelbase or six-cylinder engine and 11 ft 3½ in wheelbase. This choice of engine applied to all 1939 Lagonda models, including a new Saloon and Rapide Coupé, except for the 11 ft 6 in wheelbase Limousine by Thrupp & Maberly, which was only available with the V12. The V12 was an OHC 4480-cc (75 × 84·5 mm) unit with the two six-cylinder banks set at 60°. It developed 180 bhp at 5500 rpm.
73C: **Lanchester** Eleven Sports and Six-light Saloon sold at £295 and £298 respectively. The chassis, which had a wheelbase of 8 ft 6⅝ in, cost £220. The four-cylinder engine had a capacity of 1444 cc (66 × 105·4 mm) and was rated at 10·82 HP. Transmission was by Daimler Fluid Flywheel with pre-selective self-change four-speed gearbox (this transmission was licensed under Vulcan-Sinclair and Daimler Patents). Other 1939 Lanchesters were the Fourteen and Eighteen, both six-cylinders.

73A Humber Pullman

73B Lagonda Saloon de Ville

73C Lanchester Eleven

## 1939

74A Lea-Francis 12/14 HP

74B MG 2·6-Litre

74C Morgan 4/4

74A: **Lea-Francis** Four-light Saloon (shown) and Six-light Saloon both cost £395. A Drophead Coupé was available at £410. All had 9 ft 3 in wheelbase. Either a 12 or 14 HP engine could be ordered. They were four-cylinder Twin-OHC units of 1496-cc and 1629-cc capacity. Both had 100-mm bore, but stroke was 69 and 72 mm respectively.
74B: **MG** 2·6-Litre WA range, introduced in late 1938, supplemented the existing Midget, 1½- and 2-Litre models. It was, in fact, based on the 2-Litre SA (1936-39) but had a wider body and a 2561-cc (vs. 2322-cc) OHV six-cylinder engine which developed 100 bhp at 4400 rpm. Some 370 were produced, with Saloon (shown) and Tickford Folding Head Foursome bodywork, although a Charlesworth Tourer was advertised also.
74C: **Morgan** 4/4 had for some years been powered by a Coventry-Climax 1122-cc four-cylinder F-head engine, but in mid-1939 a new 1267-cc unit was announced. It was a 38·8-bhp OHV Four, specially made by the Standard Motor Co. This engine was continued after the war until 1950. Gearbox was four-speed, wheelbase 7 ft 8 in, tyre size 4·50-17. Shown is the Two-seater model. Morgan three-wheelers had Ford Eight and Ten engines, or 990-cc V-twin, with three-speed gearbox.
74D: **Morgan** 4/4 Four-seater Tourer was basically similar to the Two-seater but the body was somewhat longer and only one spare wheel was carried instead of two as on the Two-seater and the Drophead Coupé.

74D Morgan 4/4

75A: **Morris** 1939 line-up. From right to left are the new Eight and Ten and the Series III Twelve-Four, Fourteen-Six and Twenty-five Six, which were carryovers from 1938. In the foreground is Major Gardner's MG record breaker in which he achieved over 200 mph. Reid Railton had designed the highly efficient aero-dynamic bodywork.
75B: **Morris** Eight, Series E, had entirely new frontal appearance. The engine was an improved edition of the previous Series II 918-cc side-valve Four, but the three-speed gearbox was replaced by a four-speed. Wheelbase was one inch shorter, at 7 ft 5 in.
75C: **Morris** Eight, Series E, in Australia. This Series comprised a Two-seater, a Tourer (shown), a Two-door and a Four-door Saloon. The saloons could be ordered with sliding roof at extra cost.
75D: **Morris** Ten-Four, Series M, Saloon. This model, which cost £175, had an 1140-cc OHV four-cylinder engine, rated at 9·99 HP, a four-speed gearbox and Lockheed hydraulic brakes. Wheelbase was 7 ft 10 in, tyre size 5·00-16. Sliding roof was optional.
75E: **Riley** Twelve Model 29S Saloon had a four-cylinder 1496-cc (69 x 100 mm) OHV engine, four-speed gearbox and 9 ft wheelbase. It featured several styling modifications. A drophead coupé, Model 29D, was also available. Other 1939 Rileys were of the 16 HP type (saloon and drophead coupé).

75A Morris 1939 models

75B Morris Eight

75C Morris Eight

75D Morris Ten-Four

75E Riley Twelve

## 1939

76A: **Rolls-Royce** offered Wraith 25/30 six-cylinder and Phantom III 40/50 V-12-cylinder chassis with wheelbase lengths of 11 ft 4 in and 11 ft 10 in respectively. The chassis cost £1100 and £1900. Shown is a Brougham de Ville by Park Ward.
76B: **Rover** Twelve four-cylinder 11·9 HP Sports Saloon. Other models offered in 1939 were the Ten, Fourteen, Sixteen and Twenty. The latter three had six-cylinder engines. Saloon prices ranged from £275 (Ten) up to £425 (Twenty). The Twelve shown had 9 ft 4 in wheelbase, 5·25-17 tyres and a 1496-cc (69 × 100 mm) engine.
76C: **Singer** Nine Roadster was an attractive little sports car and had a 1074-cc (60 × 95 mm) four-cylinder power unit, rated at 8·93 HP, with three-speed gearbox. Wheelbase was 7 ft 7 in, tyre size 5·00-16. Other 1939 Singers were the Ten and Twelve models with 9·84 HP 1185-cc and 11·47 HP 1525-cc engine respectively and four-speed gearboxes.
76D: **Singer** Nine Roadster frequently appeared in sporting events. Picture shows Messrs L. Cade and R. Bicknell during the 1939 RAC Rally, negotiating a steep incline at Hastings.

76C Singer Nine

76A Rolls-Royce Phantom III

76B Rover Twelve

76D Singer Nine

77A: **SS** Jaguar Drophead Coupé was available on $3\frac{1}{2}$-, $2\frac{1}{2}$- and $1\frac{1}{2}$-Litre chassis at £465, £415 and £318 respectively. The $1\frac{1}{2}$-Litre had 9 ft $4\frac{1}{2}$ in wheelbase, 5·25-18 tyres and 1775·8-cc four-cylinder engine, the larger models had 10 ft wheelbase, 5·50-18 tyres and six-cylinder engines of 3485·5- and 2663·7-cc cubic capacity. Four-door saloons were also available on these three chassis. The 100 Le Mans type Two-seater was available only with $3\frac{1}{2}$- and $2\frac{1}{2}$-Litre engine, at £445 and £395 respectively.
77B: **Standard** Flying Eight Tourer, introduced in October 1938, was smallest of the company's range and had a 31-bhp 1021-cc (57 × 100 mm) side-valve Four engine with three-speed gearbox. Model shown cost £125. Saloon was only slightly more expensive. They featured independent front suspension with single transverse leaf spring. Wheelbase was 6 ft 11 in.

77C: **Standard** Flying Ten Super Four-door Saloon had a 1267-cc (63·5 × 100 mm) Four engine, four speeds and 7 ft 6 in wheelbase. Note the extended luggage boot.
77D: **Standard** Flying Fourteen Touring Saloon. The 1939 model range was announced in July 1938. Saloon prices ranged from £129 (8HP) up to £325 (20 HP). The 14 HP shown cost £268 and had 9 ft wheelbase.
77E: **Sunbeam-Talbot** Ten Sports Tourers were evidently popular with police forces. This batch was taken into service in Lancashire in mid-1939. They had a 9·8 HP 41-bhp 1185-cc four-cylinder side-valve engine (a tuned variant of the Hillman Minx), 7 ft 9 in wheelbase and 5·25-16 tyres.

77A SS Jaguar $3\frac{1}{2}$-Litre

77C Standard Flying Ten

77D Standard Flying Fourteen

77B Standard Flying Eight

77E Sunbeam-Talbot Ten

78A: **Sunbeam-Talbot** Ltd (formerly Clement Talbot Ltd) Motor Works at Barlby Road, Ladbroke Grove, London W10, turned out Ten, 3-Litre and 4-Litre models. New cars are seen here receiving the finishing touch before delivery.
78B: **Sunbeam-Talbot** 4-Litre chassis with Thrupp & Maberly coachwork at the Earls Court Motor Show. This car was priced at £630 and had a 4086-cc (80 × 120 mm) six-cylinder engine, rated at 26·88 HP. The chassis cost £350. The 3-Litre chassis, at £310, was similar but had 75-mm bore engine, giving 3181 cc, 20·9 HP. Both had 9 ft 10 in wheelbase and 6·25-16 tyre size. Standard saloons cost £455 and £415 respectively.
78C: **Triumph** Dolomite 14/65 Fixed-Head Roadster Coupé (of which only two were made) cost £395 and had pleasing lines. The engine was a 1767-cc Four of 13·95 HP treasury rating. Wheelbase was 9 ft, tyre size 5·00-17. The Drophead version was a consistent winner in coachwork competitions.

78C Triumph Dolomite 14/65

78A Sunbeam-Talbot

78D Vauxhall Ten

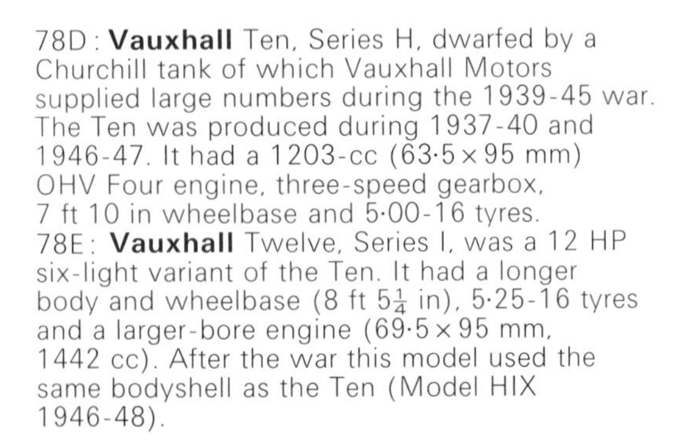

78D: **Vauxhall** Ten, Series H, dwarfed by a Churchill tank of which Vauxhall Motors supplied large numbers during the 1939-45 war. The Ten was produced during 1937-40 and 1946-47. It had a 1203-cc (63·5 × 95 mm) OHV Four engine, three-speed gearbox, 7 ft 10 in wheelbase and 5·00-16 tyres.
78E: **Vauxhall** Twelve, Series I, was a 12 HP six-light variant of the Ten. It had a longer body and wheelbase (8 ft $5\frac{1}{4}$ in), 5·25-16 tyres and a larger-bore engine (69·5 × 95 mm, 1442 cc). After the war this model used the same bodyshell as the Ten (Model HIX 1946-48).

78B Sunbeam-Talbot 4-Litre

78E Vauxhall Twelve

79A: **Vauxhall** Fourteen Six, Series J, looked like Twelve, Series I, but was slightly larger with a wheelbase of 8 ft 9 in, 5·50-16 tyres and built-out boot. Its 1781-cc (61·5 × 100 mm) six-cylinder OHV engine was good for 30 mpg and 70 mph. It was produced during 1939-40 and again during 1946-48. The Vauxhall 25 HP models (*see* 1938) were not continued after 1939.
79B: **Wolseley** Ten, Series III, was introduced early in 1939 and had a four-cylinder OHV engine, four-speed gearbox, 5·50-16 tyres and 7 ft 6 in wheelbase. It was re-introduced after the war.
79C: **Wolseley** six-cylinder models, Series III, all had OHV engines, ranging from 14 to 25 HP. Shown from left to right are the 14/60 Saloon (£285), 18/85 Saloon (£325), 25 Super Six Drop-head Coupé (£498) and the top-line 25 Super Six Limousine (£775). Wheelbase of the latter was 11 ft 9 in.

79B Wolseley Ten

79A Vauxhall Fourteen

79C Wolseley 14-25 HP

## SUMMARY OF MAJOR BRITISH CAR MAKES
**1935-1939 (with dates of their existence)**

|  |  |
|---|---|
| AC | (from 1908) |
| Alvis | (1920–67) |
| Armstrong Siddeley | (1919–60) |
| Austin | (from 1906) |
| Bentley | (from 1920) |
| Crossley | (1904–37) |
| Daimler | (from 1896) |
| Ford | (from 1911) |
| Frazer-Nash | (1924–60) |
| Hillman | (from 1907) |
| Humber | (from 1898) |
| Jowett | (1906–54) |
| Lagonda | (1906–63) |
| Lanchester | (1895–1956) |
| Lea-Francis | (1904–60)* |
| MG | (from 1924) |
| Morgan | (from 1910) |
| Morris | (from 1913) |
| Riley | (1898–1969) |
| Rolls-Royce | (from 1904) |
| Rover | (from 1904) |
| Singer | (1905–70) |
| SS (later Jaguar) | (from 1932) |
| Standard | (1903–63) |
| Sunbeam | (1899–1937)** |
| Sunbeam-Talbot | (1937–54) |
| Talbot | (1903–38) |
| Triumph | (from 1923) |
| Vauxhall | (from 1903) |
| Wolseley | (from 1911) |

*irregularly **and from 1953


## ACKNOWLEDGEMENTS

This book was compiled and written largely from historic source material in the library of the Olyslager Organisation, and in addition photographs and/or other material was kindly provided or loaned by several manufacturers and other organisations, notably:
AC Cars Ltd, Alvis Owner Club (Mr R. A. Cox), B. T. Batsford Ltd, British Leyland Motor Corp. Ltd, British Salmson Owners' Club (Mr P. A. M. Perry), Chrysler United Kingdom Ltd, Devon Vintage Car Club (Mr D. K. Myers), Dorking Motor Company Ltd, Ford Motor Company Ltd, Jaguar Cars Ltd, Morgan Motor Company Ltd, The National Motor Museum, Old Motor Magazine, The Rover Company Ltd, The Society of Motor Manufacturers and Traders Ltd, Triumph Motor Company Ltd, Triumph Owners Club (Mr A. C. Cook), Vauxhall Motors Ltd, and Wadham Stringer (Guildford) Ltd, as well as a number of private individuals, particularly Messrs L. W. Barr, G. A. Ingram and D. Lipscombe.
The Editor's special thanks are due to Michael Sedgwick; David J. Voller, John M. Carpenter and Dick Schornagel for valuable assistance rendered in collating and checking material.


## INDEX